MW01001918

Praise for Robert B. Carleson

Bob Carleson was the guiding light and hand behind the historic 1996 Welfare Reform Act. We were all standing on the shoulders of the "quiet giant." And, oh, by the way, he had provided the same leadership to Governor Reagan on his historic California Welfare Reform Act in 1971. This book is an invaluable history of an invaluable contribution to American law and human dignity.

—Tony Blankley, author of *American Grit: What It Will Take to Survive and Win in the Twenty-First Century*

Without Bob Carleson, Ronald Reagan's dream of welfare reform never would have become a reality. Bob was a man of unmatched tenacity and devotion to conservative ideals—and should be remembered as one of the most remarkable figures of our age.

—Kenneth Y. Tomlinson,
former editor in chief, *Reader's Digest*

Welfare, both its destructive tendencies and the ways it can be made to help rather than hold people back, are two of the most challenging issues in politics. Bob Carleson was present—and instrumental—at the creation of welfare reform with Ronald Reagan, when the Gipper was governor. And he pioneered many of the reforms that culminated in the pathbreaking federal welfare reform of 1996—one of the most successful public policy changes in history.

—John Fund, *Wall Street Journal*

Bob Carleson was one of this country's finest public servants—ever. A welfare reform pioneer, he enabled then-governor Ronald

Reagan to salvage California from bankruptcy—and help the desperately needy to boot. His ideas, incorporated into the hugely successful 1996 federal welfare law, were also critical in elevating Reagan into the Oval Office. Teddy Kennedy may have been the Lion of the Senate; Bob was a Lion for America.

—ALLAN H. RYSKIND, former editor and owner of *Human Events*

Bob is considered by many to be the man who had the most to do with Ronald Reagan's journey from the governorship of California to the Oval Office. As we worked together in the "Reagan Revolution," it became clear to me that Bob Carleson was no mere number-cruncher or policy wonk. . . . Carleson cared so much about the poor that he devoted the majority of his adult life to trying to reform the failed programs that were creating generational poverty and cycles of dependency. . . . And in the process he remembered that every dollar that went to help the truly needy came out of the pockets of America's taxpayers.

—GARY BAUER in the *Weekly Standard*

No one who studies the rise of modern conservatism in the latter half of the twentieth century could deny the importance of Robert B. Carleson. His tireless campaign to reform welfare stands not only as one of conservatism's first tests, but also one of its first and everlasting successes. . . . As many have remarked, without a Bob Carleson there might not have been a President Ronald Reagan. . . . But even the humble may cast large shadows, and few larger than Robert Carleson's.

—*Washington Times*

Carleson, a thoughtful public servant, didn't need the academics to teach him human nature. . . . The political historians, going back a third of a century, will find Carleson at the center of welfare reform. . . .

—*Investor's Business Daily*

Millions of Americans owe Carleson a debt of gratitude for spearheading consistently the concept of workfare. . . . Thanks in large part to Carleson's persistent prodding, the 1996 welfare reform plan enacted by the Republican-led Congress and signed into law by President Clinton instituted a block grant program, replacing federal matching grants for welfare recipients, a perverse incentive for states to keep their welfare rolls high.

—Paul M. Weyrich,
Free Congress Foundation

As Governor Reagan's welfare commissioner in Sacramento, Robert B. Carleson crafted the concept of "tough love" welfare reform. That concept enabled Reagan to take tens of thousands off the Golden State's massive relief rolls, save the state from bankruptcy and pave the way for the landmark federal welfare reform act of 1996.

—John Gizzi, *Human Events*

Bob was a key leader in Governor Reagan's effort to reform welfare, and as director of social welfare, he was the guy who had to do the hard work in the field to make sure that the governor's reforms took hold.

—James Hall, former California
Secretary of Health and Welfare

GOVERNMENT IS THE PROBLEM

Government Is the Problem

Memoirs of Ronald Reagan's
Welfare Reformer

Robert B. Carleson

Edited by
Susan A. Carleson and Hans Zeiger

Carleson, Robert

Government is the problem: memoirs of Ronald Reagan's welfare reformer / Robert B. Carleson; edited by Susan A. Carleson and Hans Zeiger. — 1st ed. — Alexandria, VA: American Civil Rights Union, c2009.

p. ; cm.

ISBN: 978-0-9786502-3-0 (13-digit ISBN); 0-9786502-3-9 (10-digit ISBN)

Includes index.

1. Carleson, Robert. 2. Public welfare—United States. 3. Public welfare administration—United States. 4. Government spending policy—United States. 5. United States—Politics and government—1981–1989. 6. United States—Politics and government—2009–

I. Carleson, Susan A. II. Zeiger, Hans.

HV95.C337 2009
361.6/80973—dc22 0911

Published in the United States by:
American Civil Rights Union
3213 Duke Street
Suite 625
Alexandria, VA 22314
wwww.theacru.org

Manufactured in the United States of America

Dedicated by the editors

to the memory of Bob Carleson.

Table of Contents

Foreword

Edwin Meese III

On Ronald Reagan's desk in Sacramento and at the White House, there was a little sign that read, "There is no limit to what you can accomplish if you don't care who gets the credit." As you might imagine, it is rare that you find somebody in Washington who abides by that maxim. There are plenty of Washington insiders who spend their days scrambling for the renown that they are certain should accompany their insignificant accomplishments. But when you finally encounter somebody who has changed the lives of millions across the country and is more concerned about the public good than public recognition, you have discovered the sort of person President Reagan had in mind when he placed that sign on his desk. Robert B. Carleson was such a man. Few Americans have done so much for the country with as little credit.

Bob Carleson spent his career as a public servant, first in the Navy during the Korean War, then as a local government administrator in California, where he learned firsthand that communities can solve many of their own problems much better than more distant policymakers in Sacramento or Washington. He did not forget that truth when he himself ended up in the state and national capitals. He never let his proximity to power spoil his common sense. Some people go to Washington and get infected with "Potomac fever." They lose sight of what is truly important in the world and begin to operate under the belief that the world revolves around the federal government in the District of Columbia. Not Bob. He, like our boss Ronald Reagan, knew that good policy was based on the best interests of the people, not the special interests.

And, as this book demonstrates, Bob was persistent. He never gave up on his goal of rescuing Americans from welfare dependency.

The nation's welfare system was a national disgrace by the late 1960s. It was a threat to the American experiment in self-government, which presupposes a certain determination among the people to work for their own welfare, to provide for their families, to improve themselves educationally and economically, to innovate and create and build an even better life for future generations. When a need arose, people looked to their family, church, and community for aid. It was understood from the time of the Founding that government was "to promote the general welfare," not to provide it. It was only with the New Deal in the 1930s that government went from promoting to providing welfare. At some point, it was no longer necessary to even qualify the word "welfare" to identify the government's role in it. Simply saying "welfare" was enough to indicate that government was the provider.

The government welfare system was increasingly harmful to the American people. It appeared to relieve them of the important tasks once undertaken by private institutions. It created a dangerous alternative to the market system of work and rewards for the nation's poor. Worst of all, it created incentives for states to increase their welfare caseloads. Through matching funds to the states, the federal government stopped promoting the general welfare, and started promoting the welfare rolls.

Ronald Reagan had little patience with the welfare-state model of government. He saw it as a serious departure from the Founders' model of limited government, federalism, and individual responsibility. "In this present crisis," Reagan declared in the midst of a recession, record inflation, high unemployment, and in the face of high taxes, bloated government, and rising welfare roles, "government is not the solution to our problem; government is the problem." Reagan labored to make government, as he said, "stand by our side, not ride on our back."

Those of us who were privileged to take part in Ronald Reagan's "revolution" knew that it would not die when he left office. In an address to Congress in 1993, even President Clinton promised to "end welfare as we know it."

The historic welfare reform of 1996 was a long time in coming. It all began in 1970, when Governor Reagan drafted Bob Carleson to design a plan to reform California's out-of-control welfare caseload. Thanks to Bob's efforts, California became a model to the rest of the nation for its ability to meet the needs of the poor by getting the non-needy off of the welfare rolls and increasing assistance to the truly needy. Bob then went on to become U.S. Commissioner of Welfare, where he pitched the California model to the other forty-nine states. When Ronald Reagan went to the White House, Bob once again provided the blueprint for additional welfare reforms. And finally, when President Clinton declared his desire to "end welfare as we know it," Bob went to work to make sure that those were not just hollow words. The resulting welfare reform passed by Congress in 1996 was described by even its critics as the greatest domestic policy reform in American history. Thanks to the restructuring of welfare, millions of Americans joined the workforce, child poverty decreased, and Americans once again could take confidence that our experiment in self-government was succeeding.

This publication of Bob Carleson's memoirs could not be more timely. The United States is in the midst of one of the largest expansions of government in our history. President Obama and the Democratic Congress have quickly—with little time for the appropriate debate about the proper role of government in our lives—provided huge welfare checks to ailing corporations and financial institutions, instituted expensive new federal programs, and issued costly new regulations. And hidden in the middle of the $787 billion "stimulus" bill passed by Congress and signed by the president in February 2009 were billions of dollars of matching funds to the states for new welfare caseloads. While no one can dispute the success of the 1996 welfare reform, advocates of a larger welfare state are doing what they can to quietly overturn that reform.

If Bob Carleson were still with us, he would be sounding the alarm. He would remind us that the welfare state destroys human dignity and human liberty. He would call us back to the Founders' vision of limited government. Fortunately, we can still benefit from Bob's wisdom and experience through this book. Robert B. Carleson's amazing legacy to America endures.

Acknowledgments

This book was on Bob's to-do list when he passed on in 2006. He left us with the early chapters of the manuscript, but it was nowhere near complete. So we began, in the fall of 2008, to piece together the chapters he had prepared for the book along with selected articles that he had written about welfare reform over the years. Though this book falls far short of what Bob intended, we are confident that it comes as close as an edited compilation permits. While merging numerous articles and essays into a single narrative, we labored to preserve Bob's original voice. We kept our editorial alterations to a minimum.

Given the use of Bob's previously published articles throughout this book, it is appropriate to acknowledge the original sources of those articles:

- "The Reagan Welfare Reforms," *The Journal, Institute for Socioeconomic Studies*, Vol. V, No. 2 (Summer 1980)
- "The Alternatives: True Reform or Federalization," *Commonsense: A Republican Journal of Thought and Opinion*, Winter 1980
- "Hamilton vs. Jefferson, 1995," *Washington Times*, March 21, 1995, A17
- "Welfare Reform: Should There Be Strings Attached?" National Center for Policy Analysis, Brief Analysis, July 11, 1995
- "Can Welfare Reform Survive Friendly Fire?" *Washington Times*, February 29, 1996, A21
- "Welfare Reform: Building on a Good Start," National Center for Policy Analysis, Brief Analysis, No. 216, November 12, 1996
- "Reagan's Vision of Welfare in America," *Washington Times*, November 24, 1996, B4
- "Welfare Reform and Income Redistribution," *Finding Our Roots, Facing Our Future: America in the Twenty-First Century*, January 1997
- "Workfare Protection Etched in Reforms," *Washington Times*, October 26, 1997, B4
- "Welfare Reform Successes," *Washington Times*, August 1, 2000, A18
- "States Handled Welfare Reform, So Why Not Use Them Again?" *Human Events* (humanevents.com) online, March 3, 2003

- "Real Welfare Reform," *Washington Times*, April 18, 2005, A19

This project would not have been possible without the hard work and dedication of Betty Barrett. Betty organized and retyped Bob's writings so that we could begin the editing process. The extraordinary Jeremy Beer skillfully shepherded the manuscript to publication. Claire Liston's talent for design is evident on the book jacket.

The Scaife Foundation and the Free Congress Foundation deserve a special word of thanks for their support of Bob's work in the 1990s when he was making the final case for welfare reform in numerous articles and speeches. The late Paul Weyrich, founder of the Free Congress Foundation, was a true champion of liberty.

Finally, the board of directors, policy board, and generous supporters of the American Civil Rights Union have made possible the continuation of Bob's legacy through the organization he founded in 1998 to "protect the civil rights of all Americans." Foremost among the friends of the American Civil Rights Union—and foremost among Bob's friends—has been Ed Meese. His generous foreword here is a blessing.

Susan A. Carleson
(Mrs. Robert B. Carleson)
Alexandria, Virginia

Hans Andreas Zeiger
Claremont, California

Introduction

"To Promote the General Welfare"

In August 1970, welfare in California was completely out of control, both in human and monetary terms. State and local budgets were gravely burdened by the need to provide funds for welfare costs. Many levels of government were being forced to freeze or cut back on important and necessary programs in order to sustain welfare's constantly rising demands.

In ten years' time, during periods of great prosperity, California's welfare rolls had soared from 600,000 to over 2.2 million persons, and the cost exceeded $2.5 billion per year (over $14 billion in 2008 dollars).[1] Welfare and fiscal experts were unanimous in predicting that, no matter what might be done, welfare's exponential growth would continue. Gigantic tax increases

1. Bureau of Labor Statistics, CPI Inflation Calculator, http://data.bls.gov/cgi-bin/cpicalc.pl, accessed September 20, 2008.

would be required. Legislative analyst A. Alan Post, in his commentary on the 1971–72 budget bill, predicted that regardless of what was done administratively or legislatively, the Aid to Families with Dependent Children (AFDC) rolls would grow by at least 500,000 persons in the succeeding two-year period. He made a very persuasive argument that history had proven that even with an improvement in the economy the rolls would continue to spiral upward.[2]

Welfare in California was administered at the county level and supervised by the state. The counties had been the bulwark of support for a healthy home rule policy but were one by one throwing up their hands and asking for the state to step in. Finally, the California County Supervisors' Association asked for the state to take over the administration of the program.

The financial squeeze was really hurting many welfare recipients. Funds had been spread so thin that those who were truly in need of assistance were receiving insufficient grants to meet their needs, while many who were better-off continued to reap regular government-issued checks.

In testimony before the U.S. Senate Finance Committee on February 1, 1972, Governor Ronald Reagan said:

> We didn't just become aware of this problem in 1970, but our earlier efforts to deal with it weren't

---

2. California Joint Legislative Budget Committee, Reg. Sess., 1971, *An Analysis of the Budget Bill of the State of California for Fiscal Year July 1, 1971–June 30, 1972: Report of the Legislative Analysts*, 686–89.

too successful. Perhaps, because we relied on professional welfare solutions and all too often they were more familiar with what they were sure they could not do, the situation became worse instead of better.

Finally, to avert a fiscal and human disaster, I asked several members of my administration, who had proven themselves in other state administrative posts, to form a task force and to devote full time for as long as it took to see if and how real reform of welfare could be developed and implemented.

In the Beginning

The task of this book is to explain what happened next—how Ronald Reagan, a handful of others, and I fixed America's broken welfare system. First, then, we have to understand what happened long before Ronald Reagan proposed reforming welfare. We need to look back a couple of centuries. America's Founders debated "the general welfare" long before we took it up in 1970s California.

In the 1790s, the Federalist and Anti-Federalist fights that resulted in the Constitution and the Bill of Rights carried over into George Washington's administration as an ongoing battle between Alexander Hamilton and Thomas Jefferson. Hamilton, the Federalist, did not trust the people and the states and therefore pressed for a strong centralized government. Jefferson, the Anti-Federalist, trusted the people and the states but did not trust a centralized government. In addition, Jefferson believed that the least government was the best government. These days, both men would be considered conservatives.

A century later, in the 1890s, the Republican Party was a Hamiltonian party that rode roughshod over the states. But the result was a great nation stretching from the Atlantic to the Pacific, connected by railroads that only a strong centralized government could have achieved.

Then, in the twentieth century, Jefferson's worst fears came true. Franklin D. Roosevelt greatly expanded the already strong central government in the name of the New Deal. Succeeding presidents, Democratic and Republican alike, continued the expansions.

Coming of age with the New Deal, Ronald Reagan started out as a big government Democrat. But as government became even bigger and more intrusive, Ronald Reagan rethought his commitment to big government. Gradually, Reagan came to the realization that Jefferson had been right, that a strong central government—no matter how well-meaning—would get out of the control of the people and into the control of unelected career bureaucrats.

Then, in the twentieth century, Jefferson's worst fears came true. Franklin D. Roosevelt greatly expanded the already strong central government in the name of the New Deal. Roosevelt and the Democrats were very clever in 1935 when they created the Aid to Families with Dependent Children program, what we commonly called welfare. They simply made it an open-ended, state-administered entitlement program, with the states setting the eligibility requirements and benefit levels. The federal government automatically matched whatever a state spent. All states got a dollar-for-dollar match, and the states with a greater number of poor families got a greater percentage match. Since that time, other programs have been created using the same principle. Medicaid and the old social services program are examples.

When he became president, Reagan was faced with seemingly conflicting goals. First, he aimed to rebuild our defenses to prove to the Soviet Union and to the world that socialism could not compete with a democratic free market system. He called for the collapse of the "evil empire" that had threatened the world for more than forty years. This required a strong central government. Reagan's second goal was to return the country to a Jeffersonian ideal of smaller, decentralized government centered in the states.

Actually, both goals were consistent with Jefferson's idea of government. Jefferson believed in a strong national defense provided by the national government. This was consistent with his conviction that in other matters the people, through the states, should prevail.

Reagan chose to address the threat to world security as his first priority. A Congress controlled by the Democratic Party, which believed in the expansion of the centralized welfare state, often held his defense buildup hostage to an expansion of the welfare state. But despite the political challenges he faced, Ronald Reagan's goal of eliminating Soviet communism was realized.

And Reagan's legacy continued. In 1994, the voters sent a new generation of Republicans to the governors' mansions. The voters overturned the longtime

Democrat-party rule in Congress, and elected a new Republican majority. With both houses of Congress in conservative hands, we could finally realize Reagan's Jeffersonian goals: a strong national defense and a smaller, state-based government of the people.

However, as in 1795, in 1995 the conservatives were split between the "Hamiltonians," who did *not* trust the states and the people to "do the right thing," and the "Jeffersonians," who did trust the states and the people. The modern "Jeffersonians" did not trust unelected federal bureaucrats to take charge of implementing reforms in the welfare system.

The issue of block-granting welfare was a prime example. We heard the phrases "we must fix it before we send it back" and "we raised the money, we should say how it is spent." Those who held these views were philosophical descendants of Hamilton—they did not trust the states and the people.

Ronald Reagan, like Jefferson, trusted the states and the people to ensure that state officials "do the right thing." Reagan had experienced how federal bureaucrats who write the regulations implementing tough laws can turn them into weak, ineffective reversals of what the legislators intended, thereby preempting state interpretations. But above all, he believed that the federal government should not be dictating to the states. He disagreed with the followers of Hamilton who told us that the national government knew best.

Of course, such voices are still very much with us. We must be reminded why they are so wrong. We must learn why, after all, welfare reform worked.

1

The Birth of True Welfare Reform

I was lying on the sand of Capistrano Beach, California, my first vacation in four years. But I was not really on vacation. It was a Saturday, and I was poring through a volume of the Health and Welfare Code of the State of California with a recording device at my side. There the recorder sat, waiting patiently for my dictation, but nothing came. Sunday night I was to fly back to Sacramento, leaving my family to their true vacation on the beach. I had been drafted into this mess by that master salesman, Ronald Reagan.

It all started one week before, in August 1970. I was about to leave on the long-deferred vacation with my family, two weeks at the beach. I told my secretary that nothing would stop me from this respite from responsibility. "Nothing?" she replied, "not even the governor?"

"Well," I responded confidently, "Of course, if Ronald Reagan called, I would come; but he won't call." In my two years as number two in what was to become the California Department of Transportation, I had briefed Governor Reagan several times on highway matters, but nothing was pending, and we weren't expecting any earthquakes.

Much to my surprise, another sort of quake did hit, and I was called to the governor's office. We met in Reagan's capitol suite. Four of us from his administration had been handpicked to serve as a welfare task force, one of us from the governor's office and one each from three of four cabinet agencies, the excepted fourth being the agency that contained the Department of Social Welfare. We were to start immediately and devote ourselves full time to this effort. While others in our departments would carry our regular loads, our task force was to be secret, because the governor did not want our work to become a political football in the middle of his campaign for reelection. I could return to my office each evening to sign necessary papers, but otherwise my time and attention would be directed to the arcane subject of welfare.

Governor Reagan told us that welfare spending was out of control. We were in the second year of a freeze on additional state spending because of welfare costs. All other state functions, including education, were taking a back seat to welfare. If Reagan were reelected, he would need a welfare reform plan. If not, he would leave it to his successor.

I had been nominated to the task force by James M. Hall, secretary of the business and transportation agency in which the Department of Public Works was located. I have long since forgiven Jim for inflicting welfare on me, but I would never have chosen to "get into welfare" under any other circumstances. Those of us who really knew and therefore respected Ronald Reagan would never say no to his request. He had long since earned my respect.

Getting to Know Ronald Reagan

My interest in government began when my father was elected to the city council of Long Beach, California, in 1947. I was sixteen years old and attended a few city council meetings, ostensibly to meet high school requirements, but in reality, it was to see my father in action. At those meetings, I noticed that the mayor and council listened to a man called the "city manager." He made recommendations, and the council always seemed to act on them. He was the chief executive officer, and they were the board of directors. He appointed the chief of police, the fire chief, the city engineer, and all other department heads; he prepared and submitted the budget, but he received little publicity—that went to the mayor and council. They were part-time, he was full-time. Then and there I decided that I wanted to be a city manager.

First, I needed to fulfill an ambition that virtually all Long Beach teenagers who had lived through World War II had: to become a naval officer. We were all patriots at that time. I earned a naval scholarship to the

University of Utah, and two years later transferred to the University of Southern California's School of Public Administration, the professional training ground for California's city managers. After graduation, I fulfilled my naval obligation in Korea, and at sea on the heavy cruiser *Bremerton* and with the First Marine Division.

In June 1956, I embarked, finally, on my city manager career by becoming the part-time administrative intern to the city administrator of Beverly Hills, California, while doing post graduate work at USC. Later, I served as administrative assistant to the Beverly Hills director of public works. I then served successively as city clerk and assistant to the city manager of Claremont, California, and senior administrative assistant to the city manager of Torrance, California.

In October 1960, at the age of twenty-nine, I was appointed the first city manager of the newly incorporated city of San Dimas, California—thirteen years after deciding to make city management my career. I was on my way, I hoped, to becoming the city manager of Long Beach or San Diego, the premier professional manager cities of that day.

I left my career in city management reluctantly in December 1968 to assume the chief deputy director position at the California Department of Public Works. This was a major career opportunity for me, but I had some hesitation due to what I had seen and learned while serving as an assistant with the city of Beverly Hills, where I had come in contact with many Hollywood actors. Almost all I had met were vacuous and dim. I had not met Ronald Reagan, but I feared that he would be like them. I was concerned by press reports that he was just an actor and was directed by others. I had voted for him, but I had yet to be convinced that he was different from the actors I had met. His strong stand against student radicals at the University of California impressed me, though, so I decided to accept the offer by the newly promoted director of the department, Jim Moe, to help him run a department that I had had to deal with, sometimes contentiously, during my eight years as a city manager.

Shortly after I arrived in Sacramento in January 1969, I was introduced formally to Governor Reagan in his office. But I really did not get to see him up close and in action until the great floods of northern California in the 1969–70 winter storm season. I had been selected to brief him and present our recommendation for repairing the massive damage done to highways and bridges in the north. I was alone with him in his small private office, and nervous. I presented a chart listing the cost to repair the damage, county by county. I presented our finding that current gas tax revenues could not cover the cost and gave him our recommendation that a temporary six month gas tax increase of two cents per gallon would be necessary.

From the moment I began, Reagan peered from behind his half glasses as he read the briefing paper and asked good, deep questions about the extent and types of damage in the counties. When I got to the temporary increase in the gas tax, he frowned and commented that he was opposed to tax increases. I said that I was too, but the gas tax came only from highway users and would be spent only to repair their highways. He asked, "How do we know we need two cents for six months?"

I responded that the engineers and accountants in our department had reported these findings.

"Well," he said, "I know those guys are conservative in their estimates. Why don't we make it an increase for a *maximum* of six months, with the governor given the authority to end it sooner if enough revenue comes in before then?"

I quickly saw his point and agreed. Why hadn't we thought of that? (The emergency legislation was passed Reagan's way and the gas tax was ended in four months.)

No presentations had been made to him before mine. I had brought the briefing paper with me because a special press conference was to follow immediately after the briefing, and we were unable to get it to him sooner. I was alone with him. It was his idea, quick and on the spot.

At a press conference following my briefing, a smart aleck in the capitol press corps asked him, "Governor, how much storm damage occurred in (such and such a) county?"

Reagan hesitated. I was behind the press corps and could see his eyes; he was reading our chart, which was back in his private office.

"It was 2.1 million dollars," he said. He had hit it right on the nose.

Most of the Hollywood actors I had met had good memories, but they were not smart. Ronald Reagan was both smart and creative, *and* he had photographic memory. I had underestimated him, as many "smart" people had done before me, and, as history will record, many people will do after me. That is how Ronald Reagan earned my respect. Later events would confirm this respect. To this day, when I hear someone deride Reagan's intellect, I simply ask, "Did you know him?" Invariably the answer is, "Well, no, but . . . ."

How Things Worked in Sacramento

Ronald Reagan worked largely through a "cabinet process." This process was quite different from the federal cabinet. During his campaign for governor, he had criticized his predecessor's creation of superagency heads, positions that interposed between the governor and the operating departments, and had promised to abolish them. He replaced them with four cabinet secretaries who, unlike federal cabinet members, were not involved in day-to-day management of the departments grouped under them. They were to be conduits for policy to pass from the departments to the governor, and from the governor to the departments. While the department heads worked for the governor, they reported to him through one of the cabinet secretaries. The cabinet consisted of the four secretaries, the director of finance, the lieutenant governor, and the chief of staff.

The cabinet met with the governor two or three times a week for several hours at a time. Items on the agenda were placed there by cabinet members, who frequently forwarded major issues from the departments or issues between departments that could not or should not be resolved by the respective secretaries. This was the best forum for Reagan-style decision-making. All members of the cabinet were equals on any issue to come before the cabinet. For example, the resources secretary might oppose the proposed Southern Crossing bridge over San Francisco Bay, and the business and transportation secretary might speak out about a welfare issue. Efforts to stifle debate or make log-rolling deals with each other were out of bounds; most important, after a decision was made by the governor, no one would undermine it.

One-page summaries of each agenda issue would go to the governor and cabinet well before the meeting. They could and often would be backed up by more detailed documents. The governor and members were expected to be prepared to discuss each issue at the meetings. A presentation frequently would be made by the department head or chief deputy bringing the issue, and questions and answers would follow. The members of the cabinet would give their views, and the governor would listen and make inquiries. Then discussion would be closed, and the governor usually would make a decision at the meeting, though sometimes he would take the issue under advisement and make the decision later. The important thing is that Reagan heard the arguments for and against the various options on each issue, and after every decision was made the cabinet and department heads would support it.

This kind of process works only if the members of the cabinet and administration are loyal to the governor and share his views on public policy. This is why it is so important that major appointments go to persons who can give this loyalty with enthusiasm. If a member felt that he could not support the decision, but did not have any responsibility in its implementation, then he could keep silent. If he had a responsibility to implement the decision but could not do so, then he should resign. The governor alone is elected by the people to make major decisions. All others in the administration are responsible for advising or implementing, or both.

I attended meetings in California, and later in the White House, where all persons in the meeting, except one, were on one side of an issue—and Reagan came down on the side of the individual who was on the other side. He was a man of independent judgment when he had been exposed to all sides of an argument. He did not just go with the crowd, if he thought them wrong.

The Secret Welfare Task Force

My weekend at Capistrano Beach was frustrating and wasted. Back in Sacramento on Monday, I found that the other task force members wanted to conduct hundreds of interviews with workers in the welfare system. I felt that there was a better way to accomplish our mission and I received permission from the other members to create my own subtask force.

The director of agriculture, Jerry Fielding, was the strongest supporter for my subtask force. He had been assigned the hopeless task of contacting officials in the federal Department of Health, Education, and Welfare (HEW). The other members of the task force, Ned Hutchinson, the governor's appointments secretary, and John Mayfield, deputy director of the Department of Conservation, continued with their plan for interviews.

To round out my subtask force I selected from the public works department a young lawyer named

Ronald Zumbrun and a young administrative analyst named John Svahn. I assured them that if they accepted the assignment they and I would in all probability be on a suicide mission. I chose them carefully, and they eagerly agreed. (As it turned out for Ron and John, the mission was far from suicidal: Zumbrun eventually became president of the successful Pacific Legal Foundation, and Svahn became successively the commissioner of social security, undersecretary of the Department of Health and Human Services, and assistant to the president for policy development in the Reagan administration.) With a secretary completing the team, we set ourselves up in a single room in the public works building.

We were not to be "briefed" by people working in the welfare department. We would read the laws, regulations, and court decisions relating to welfare ourselves. As I expected, the "lore" did not match the "law."

We found that the welfare system was a horrible mess. Many state and federal laws had been broadened, expanded, and twisted by implementing regulations. Many "interpretations" of federal and state laws were being made by social work professionals who gained this knowledge on a word-of-mouth basis. Often, opinions were not based on legal research.

We found that the state law had been written very generally, giving final authority to the director of the Department of Social Welfare to interpret the law and issue regulations accordingly. In the past, this authority had resided in a social welfare board. But Governor Pat Brown had requested the liberal legislature to transfer the power to the director, making the social welfare board merely advisory, and therefore toothless.

Since then, the directors had used their discretion solely to broaden eligibility for welfare benefits. For example, work-related expense deductions were accepted for everything from hairdos to telephones to automobiles—whether or not they were necessary for work. These deductions, in combination with the federally mandated work incentive income disregards, permitted thousands of non-needy persons to be on the welfare rolls by reducing their apparent earned income. "Special needs," which provided benefits in addition to the regular monthly benefits provided by law, were defined to include new or used furniture and other expensive household furnishings, including TVs.

These regulations were a gold mine of opportunity for us reformers. We could save vast sums of money for the taxpayers without hurting the truly needy.

We found that the principal welfare programs—Aid to Families with Dependent Children (AFDC) and Aid to the Aged, Blind, and Disabled (AABD)—were all open-ended entitlement programs. Federal and state funds flowed without appropriation. The more the state spent, the more federal money rolled in. But the state was going broke.

We found that the federal laws permitted state *discretion*, which, according to the conventional wisdom provided by federal and state welfare bureaucrats, were federal *requirements*.

I had made the correct decision to read the law and not be briefed by the bureaucrats.

And things were even worse than we thought. We found that the welfare system, which originally had been primarily intended to provide social services to people, had grown into a huge fiscal operation where 80 percent of the money spent was in the form of unrestricted, direct money grants to welfare recipients. Expenditures for social services accounted for only 20 percent of the total welfare budget.

Welfare laws and regulations had originally been written with the assumption that professional social workers would utilize discretion in determining eligibility and the amount of grants. But federal and state courts had consistently struck down this discretion. Courts had determined that any basis for asserting an individual's eligibility for benefits was to be translated as his inalterable right to eligibility and a maximum grant. The welfare laws were laced with gaping loopholes.

So much money was being diverted to the non-needy that the truly needy families had not seen a cost of living increase for twelve years—eight years of Pat Brown and four years of Ronald Reagan. The legislature and the governors could not increase benefits while all other state programs were suffering. The welfare bureaucrats were using their authority to broaden eligibility and special needs regulations, on top of the fact they did not check and verify eligibility. All of these factors and more resulted in automatic increases in state and federal welfare spending. This situation was not only hurting the taxpayers and other state programs, it was hurting the truly needy families for which the welfare system was created in the first place.

In December 1970, I reported to Governor Reagan that we had bad news and good news. The bad news was that the welfare situation was worse than we had thought originally. Not only were the rolls and costs growing at an uncontrolled rate, but the needy welfare families who, through no fault of their own, had to rely exclusively on public assistance to meet their basic needs had not seen a benefit increase in thirteen years. It would take an increase of more than 25 percent in basic AFDC benefits levels to close their need gap.

However, the good news was that I was convinced that, despite the conventional wisdom of the welfare establishment, there was enough waste in the system that we could meet the twin goals of (1) halting the growth in rolls and (2) increasing benefits to the truly needy.

From that day on, only Governor Reagan and a few of us in the administration really believed that these goals were possible to achieve.

2

The Work Begins

Late in December, Governor Reagan announced my appointment as director of the Department of Social Welfare, to coincide with the start of his second term in the first week of January 1971. The governor made clear his mandate: that we design and implement a comprehensive welfare reform program that would stop the growth of California's welfare rolls and generate savings that could be used to increase benefits to needy families as well as to the aged, blind, and disabled.

I appointed Zumbrun as deputy director for legal affairs and Svahn, who was too young to meet the minimum requirements for a deputy position, as assistant director for administration. I brought Carl Williams over from the Department of Public Works as assistant to Svahn. I chose Charles Hobbs as deputy director of operations. Once again, none of the members of this top team was from the welfare establishment.

We began the process immediately, by issuing emergency regulations tightening the eligibility and grant regulations. Assisting me in this process was a secret advisory group consisting of three county welfare directors and two representatives from county administrators' offices. They were people I trusted. Their job was to advise me if an emergency regulation I was intending to issue would cause an unexpected problem. I assured them that I was taking the responsibility for the regulations. I did not expect them to agree with me regarding the policy involved in the proposed regulation, but I did count on them to warn me of its consequences at the county level. This group was kept secret to protect them from reprisals from opponents of our reform efforts. The members from the county administrator's offices came from Alameda and Los Angeles counties and were selected by the respective chief administrative officers (CAOs). Arthur Will Jr. of Los Angeles County, an old friend from city manager days, selected Keith Comrie to serve on the secret advisory group. Keith would quickly rise to direct the Los Angeles County Department of Public Social Services before serving as CAO himself.

I ordered the counties to establish checking and verification procedures and developed a sixteen-page application for AFDC. Critics of welfare reform attacked the new application, which replaced a simple four-page form, by claiming that it would take hours for an applicant to complete. I responded that an applicant without assets and various forms of income could complete the form easily—most questions would simply be answered no and the entries left blank. Only applicants with many assets and many forms of income would need much time to fill out the forms. All would be signing the forms under penalty of perjury and would be responsible for the accuracy of the forms. I created a welfare fraud unit in my department, too, which eventually led to the creation of the National Welfare Fraud Association.

I had realized during our task force efforts that the absent fathers of AFDC families were getting off scot-free. The position of the Department of Health, Education, and Welfare at the time was that the fathers had no money—that they were so poor that the mothers had to leave them. I suspected otherwise. I believed that in many cases the fathers were not really absent, and that many more were "in the neighborhood." The prevailing judgment of the welfare establishment was that it would cost much more to go after the absent fathers than it would be worth. I thought not.

In California, the responsibility for enforcing child support rested with district attorneys. Child support enforcement for AFDC cases had no priority. Murder, felonies, and other priorities came before child support, as they probably should have, but virtually nothing was being done. After all, welfare was taking care of the problem, and, of course, the supposed child supporters couldn't put up the money anyway. The DAs were elected officials, as were the county supervisors, and they would have to supply the funding for an AFDC child-support enforcement effort.

I approached the district attorney's office of Sacramento county with a proposal. If Sacramento county would establish an active effort of child-support enforcement of AFDC cases, and the funds recovered from the absent parents did not equal the new costs to the county, my department would finance the shortfall. If there were no shortfall, the county could keep a major portion of the excess amount collected as a reward to be used to offset some of the county's AFDC costs. The county could not lose, but I was sure enough of the outcome to be willing to risk about $300,000 from my budget for this project. The district attorney accepted my offer.

And I was proven right. For every dollar spent on child-support enforcement in AFDC cases, three dollars was returned. We had proven the conventional wisdom wrong. This success led to the child-support enforcement incentive program, a part of the California welfare reform legislation, and later the model for Senator Russell Long's (D-LA) federal Child Support Enforcement Act (Title 4d of the Social Security Act of 1975).

Total Strategy

Ronald Reagan's welfare reform program was to be a total strategy. Our stated objectives were to:

1. Cap the uncontrolled growth in the cost of welfare,
2. Reduce the rolls to those strictly entitled to be there,

3. Reform the state/county system for the administration of the program in the future,
4. Require those able to work to do so or to seek work,
5. Increase assistance to the truly needy, and
6. Strengthen family responsibility.

Each of the major objectives was planned to be achieved by administrative, regulatory, or legislative substrategies. Many of these substrategies interlocked and served more than one objective, and thus were interdependent. Most of the administrative and regulatory changes could commence at once, without need to wait for authorizing legislation. The subsequent legislative portion of the reform closed some eligibility loopholes not able to be legally accomplished by regulation alone. In addition, the legislation served to make the welfare reforms more permanent by locking into statutory form many of the regulatory reforms initiated in early 1971 under administrative authority residing in the office of the director of the Department of Social Welfare.

During our work in the task force, we found that the director had powerful legal authority conferred by statute to determine welfare eligibility requirements based on broad legislative direction. In past years, this authority had been used by directors to expand and liberalize eligibility requirements. We had a different approach. From our point of view, these were "loopholes" to be closed to the extent they provided benefits to the non-needy.

Early in 1971, the new management team embarked on a comprehensive program to reorganize the department. We instituted scores of administrative and regulatory changes, many of which were ready for immediate implementation because of our planning during the task force. The reforms were to: (a) establish tighter eligibility standards so as to assure that only the truly needy received public assistance, and (b) change organizational and administrative procedures in order to simplify the system and prevent, as well as correct, abuses. Special attention was given to the initial eligibility determination process; it is easier to keep non-needy persons off the rolls in the first place than to remove them once they begin to receive benefits.

I requested a team of auditors brought in from the state Department of Finance to review the effectiveness of the eligibility process at both the state and county levels. They found that the state was losing over $50 million a year through eligibility errors alone.

As a result of this study, a program was developed in the department and assigned to the fiscal division to provide for the first time an audit of the eligibility system from the county down to the recipient. The reorganization brought in fiscally and administratively trained persons to operate the payment system process.

Other administrative actions to remold California's public assistance program were implemented to:

- Develop a general grant computation formula, thereby reducing local administrative problems, minimizing inequities caused by misinterpretation and eliminating overpayments;

- Clarify guidelines for "special needs" determination;
- Tighten definitions of unemployment and total disability;
- Close loopholes in welfare determination on such issues as work-related expenses, multiple grant sources, and the "two unit family," and to tighten rules governing treatment of property and other resources by recipients;
- Separate employables from unemployables and emphasize requirements;
- Require that employable benefits recipients actively seek work;
- Strengthen efforts to enhance support responsibility of absent fathers, stepfathers, and responsible relatives; and
- Crack down on welfare fraud, especially in the reporting of outside earnings, through an automated earnings clearance system.

We also increased the number of attorneys in the department to assure that answers given to counties were based on legal research rather than on the "historic knowledge" of social work professionals. Moreover, several surplus middle and upper-level management positions in the social service categories were abolished and the incumbents demoted. Even though there were a significant number of demotions, because of vacancies caused by attrition, actual layoffs were not necessary.

Of course, almost every action we took to reorganize the department and to reassign social work professionals met legal opposition from social workers' unions and other organizations representing the welfare bureaucracy. In fact, an attempt was made to destroy the new organization in the last hours of the legislature's consideration of the state budget. Fortunately, this maneuver was uncovered in time and corrective legislation followed. Nonetheless, this effort to thwart the welfare reform did serve to delay reorganizational efforts by one or two months.

In general, we reversed the philosophy of the state Department of Social Welfare. Meanwhile, we informed the counties that we expected their eligibility and grant processes to be accurate and fair, and that there would be tighter audits. They were assured that the department would back them when they took a firm position regarding the tight administration of these welfare programs.

While this broad scale administrative tightening was underway, January and February of 1971 were also busy with further formulation of a comprehensive welfare reform program based upon the data, information, and proposals generated earlier by the task force.

Driving Bob Moretti Up the Wall

We completed our work on the proposed welfare reform legislation in late February. In a historic break with tradition, the Democratic legislative leadership refused the governor permission to address the legislature to present his comprehensive welfare reform program. They claimed it would not include specifics, but would be the same old generalities—and a waste of their time. The legislature could not have been more wrong.[1]

After the legislation was rejected by the state legislature, Governor Reagan addressed the people of California on television before the town hall of Los Angeles, on March 3, 1971. The proposal presented to the people that day consisted of a book containing over 175 pages. The comprehensive reform program comprised seventy major provisions, each articulated into many subprovisions. The plan encompassed complex administrative changes, regulatory changes, and proposed legislative changes. Aggregated, they pointed to a potential annual savings of over $600 million in welfare spending. The book laid out Reagan's complete reforms, including the administrative and regulatory changes already under way, and it told how his legislative proposals dovetailed with the regulatory efforts.

In short, it was the most comprehensive and detailed welfare reform program proposed by any governor to any state in history.

Reagan's welfare reform proposal was denounced by the legislature's Democratic leadership before they had even had a chance to read it. It was quickly killed by the first legislative committee, Senator Anthony Beilenson's Health and Welfare Committee.

Reagan had anticipated this result and planned a campaign to get the legislature to capitulate or else. The "or else" was a secret initiative petition that we

---

1. See Governor Reagan's handwritten note, included in the first photo section in this book.

had prepared. The petition would be submitted to the people, and after enough signatures had been acquired, it would be submitted for the primary election ballot of 1972. Reagan would lead the charge, and since the issue would be voted on at the primary election, there would be primary opponents of Republican legislators and of Democrats in conservative Democratic districts who were not supportive or who had actively opposed welfare reform.

The Republican opponents of our welfare reform were led by Assemblyman William Bagley, chairman of the assembly welfare committee, who had been appointed by the speaker, Democrat Bob Moretti. Bagley was an ally of Jack Veneman, his predecessor as welfare committee chairman. Veneman, another Republican, had been appointed by Richard Nixon as undersecretary of the Department of Health, Education, and Welfare, and he was a point man for the Nixon Family Assistance Plan (FAP) in Washington. FAP was a guaranteed-income plan that would move welfare from the states to complete federal control and administration. It was strongly opposed by Reagan. Supporters of FAP knew that if Reagan succeeded in welfare reform in California, the largest state, their efforts to nationalize welfare were dead. Therefore, we were fighting not only the Democrats in Sacramento; we were fighting the Nixon Republicans in Sacramento and Washington. This situation made a Reagan-led welfare reform initiative in the 1972 primary election a threat to all of his opponents—Democrat and Republican, state and federal. We code-named the secret initiative plan "Operation Crossfire."

The state chamber of commerce was an ally of the governor. It was staffed with loaned executives across 120 local citizens' welfare reform committees throughout California. The activities of these committees were coordinated by a state-wide bipartisan citizens' committee chaired by Al McCandless, chairman of the board of supervisors of Riverside County, and later a longtime member of Congress. The chamber of commerce produced a brochure outlining the elements of Reagan's welfare reform. It included a quote from President Franklin Roosevelt that welfare was a "subtle narcotic to the human soul." The brochure urged voters to send an attached form to their state legislator demanding welfare reform. Many thousands of forms were sent by voters. The principal author of the Reagan legislation, state senator (and later congressman) Clair Burgener, alone received over 3,000 forms. Many more than that went to the legislators who opposed the bill. Pressure was building, particularly on Democratic senators and assemblymen from conservative, rural districts. Then, someone on the governor's staff leaked to Bill Bagley the existence of Operation Crossfire. Now the pressure was on the Republican friends of Bagley and Veneman as well. The impasse was over. Speaker Moretti himself offered to negotiate welfare reform with the governor.

Bob Moretti was a loyal Democrat, but we believed that he would support our kind of welfare reform once he saw that it was common sense—not cruel and inhumane as our left-wing opponents claimed. Moretti was a public accountant by profession, and we felt that we could negotiate with him.

The problem was that Beilenson and Bagley did not want a successful California welfare reform. Bagley had sown doubt among many Republican legislators that our reforms would work. Senator Beilenson and Assemblyman John Burton, who was chairman of the Ways and Means subcommittee under which the welfare budget fell, had controlled the debate on the Democratic side. John Burton's brother, Congressman Phil Burton, was Jack Veneman's ally in the Congress in support of Nixon's FAP.

When Moretti entered the action, real negotiations began. Fear of a popular welfare reform initiative during the primary election, led by a popular Governor Reagan, tamed the legislature.

Ronald Reagan was an accomplished negotiator. He had honed his skills as president of the Screen Actors' Guild. He had taken on studio bosses, the Communist Party, and the mafia. He was about to prove that he could do the same with a hostile legislative negotiating team. Moretti and his team made the same mistake many others had made before him and many others would make after, including Mikhail Gorbachev: They underestimated Ronald Reagan.

Since the meetings were taking place in the governor's office and Reagan had proposed the welfare reform, I urged the governor to insist on our bill as the basis of negotiations. Moretti agreed to this, thus giving us an invaluable advantage in dealing with a man who had been trained in the accounting profession, and thus would respond to the common sense of our proposals.

Next, we devised a strategy for securing the parts of the bill that we considered essential to the success of the reform. Using hidden symbols, I encoded two copies of our bill to indicate which items were absolutely necessary for welfare reform, which items would be very desirable, and last, which items could be given up without hurting our reforms. The latter were called "throw away" items. We included these items in our proposed legislation specifically for this purpose: to let the other side think that they had got something from the negotiations. One encoded copy of the bill was held by Reagan, the other by me. No one else knew of the coding system except my deputy director for legal affairs, Ronald Zumbrun, and my closest ally in the governor's cabinet, James M. Hall.

At the appointed hour, the governor seated himself at the head of the table with me to his immediate right. Speaker Moretti sat to his immediate left, with the speaker's team ranging down the table, including Republican assemblyman Bagley. At first Moretti attempted to unsettle the governor by punctuating his statements with what he thought would be shocking profanity. Governor Reagan, a real gentleman in public or in the company of women, could swear with the best of us in private, if there were no women present. There were no women present in the welfare negotiations, so he shocked Moretti and his cohorts by giving as well as he got. Their first attempt to get the better of Ronald Reagan backfired on them.

At the rear of the room sat Earl Brian. He had nothing to do with welfare reform, but as director of the Department of Health Care Services, he had negotiated a Medicaid reform with Moretti that Governor Reagan announced several years later to be a complete failure.

Early in the meeting, Brian attempted to intervene for the reform by blurting out, "Bob [Moretti], why don't we just cut this meeting short by splitting the difference in costs?" Moretti looked interested, but I was shocked and appalled. Fortunately, the governor did not fall for this suggestion, since I had briefed him on the necessity for key policy changes in the welfare reform. Later, during a break, Hall ordered Brian to leave the meeting and not come back. (When Brian ran for the U.S. Senate in 1994, he claimed untruthfully to have been the author of welfare reform. Brian was defeated in the primary. Much later, in May 1997, he was sentenced to serve fifty-seven months in federal prison for fraud in his business efforts. Hall and I had seen it coming.)

The Bridge Theory of Negotiations

This attempt by Brian to reach a quick and easy solution to the complicated issue of welfare reform is exactly why many Republican reform efforts have failed. I call it "The Bridge Theory of Negotiations."

Let's say that a new welfare policy is like a bridge which must span a 100-foot canyon. To be *most* effective, the bridge would be forty feet wide, but we could do the job with a twenty-foot-wide bridge. Now let us assume that our opponents know these facts and are trying to make our reform ineffective. Let us also assume that our principal negotiator is not expert in the details of our welfare reform proposal. Our opponent offers him 90 percent of what we want, but the offer is only ninety feet of bridge, forty feet wide. We still need ten more feet lengthwise. To our unknowledgeable negotiator this seems like a fair offer: 90 percent of what we asked for. He accepts, and the reform fails.

On the other hand, if he had known the true needs of our proposed policy, he could have counteroffered with 50 percent of our original proposal—as long as the counteroffer was expressed as a bridge 100 feet in length, but only twenty feet in width, instead of forty. The chasm would be spanned, and the policy would be a success. What had been a failure at 90 percent could be a success at 50 percent. Too often in negotiations, Republicans unschooled in the nuances of arcane welfare policy are "taken to the cleaners" by Democrats who have specialized in the subject and know how to give us 90 percent of what we ask for—in a way that will doom our efforts.

In the case of the welfare reform negotiations in Governor Reagan's office, the usual positions were reversed. Reagan knew the intricate meaning of our reforms, and Moretti did not. Neither did Brian, who would have negotiated a compromise based on mere budget numbers. If Reagan had followed his advice we would have failed. The lessons of 1971 are good years later. Budget numbers should not guide policy, especially not in welfare reform.

In our negotiations, Reagan and I followed the script. I presented each item. I framed the items that were absolutely necessary as simple changes which should not be controversial. The governor would ask Moretti if he had any objection; being none we would move on. When I came to a "throw-away" item, I would give an impassioned statement pointing out why this item was important to us. Moretti would become interested and question the need for the item. I would repeat my impassioned plea. Moretti would declare that he could not accept that item. Reagan would "try" to convince me that we should give on this item if we wanted to move on, and I would acquiesce reluctantly. On the items that we wanted but did not absolutely need, I would make a good argument and Reagan would tell Moretti that it was our turn to win one. Moretti would agree.

This negotiation went on for five days. We won, hands down. We got over 80 percent of what we proposed and all of the important elements. In former governor Pat Brown's book about Reagan, he quoted Moretti's reflections on the negotiations: "Carleson drove me up the wall." Later, in his biography of Ronald Reagan as governor, Lou Cannon repeated the Moretti quote and observed, correctly, that I was playing the bad cop to Reagan's good cop.

I also played the bad cop to Chief of Staff Edwin Meese III's good cop in the second and crucial phase of the negotiations the following week.

It was when the negotiations between Reagan and Moretti were over, and the success of welfare reform was announced jointly to the public, that the real fight began. Staff members of the legislative welfare committee understood the real effect of our victory. They had sat behind Moretti, stunned as he agreed with all of our important items. Now they were given the task of preparing the final agreed-upon legislation.

Skullduggery Afoot

On Saturday, the day after negotiations ended, Zumbrun and I were waiting in my office for the completed legislative document to arrive from the capitol. The committee staff's work was simple; we had been working from our reform bill and the changes agreed to were relatively few. But we waited, and waited. Suddenly, I told Zumbrun that we would go over to the capitol and find the legislation.

It being Saturday, only the first floor of offices was open to the public. People who were not government employees or family members were prohibited on the other floors. We went to the second floor to look for life. We heard a door slam down the hall. It was the door to the supposedly nonpartisan legislative counsel's offices. We went through the unlocked door and down a hall of empty offices, until we arrived at a closed door where we could hear voices coming from within. We opened the door. In the room were several of the welfare committee staff members, a deputy legislative counsel, and Ralph Abascal, the head of San Francisco Neighborhood Legal Assistance. Abascal was the lawyer for the plaintiff in many lawsuits against the state of California in welfare matters. He would later conduct many lawsuits challenging the law that he was now in the act of trying to craft to his purposes.

We caught the legislative staff red-handed. Abascal was not legally permitted in those offices on a Saturday. The legislative counsel was supposed to be nonpartisan. Instead, the counsel was party to the effort to subvert the agreed-upon reform legislation.

The staff tried to say that their version was the correct one. We pointed out, however, that our opponent in court had been brought in to "revise" the agreed-upon bill. I reported our discovery to Ed Meese. Bob Moretti was informed. Moretti was an honorable man. He believed that his word was his bond, but the welfare committee staff was claiming that we were the ones who were wrong. Our discovery of the Saturday meeting in the capitol gave him pause. It seemed that the agreement announced with much fanfare on Friday was blowing up on Saturday.

It was decided that members of the original negotiation teams, without the principals, Reagan and Moretti, would meet to resolve the issues. The legislative team was led by Assemblyman Leo McCarthy and the governor's team by Ed Meese. I sat to Meese's right and Zumbrun to his left on one side of the table; McCarthy sat across from Meese and was flanked by assemblymen John Burton and Bill Bagley and Senator Anthony Beilenson. We proceeded to go through the "revised" bill point by point, calling out what I referred to as legal "land mines" that had been put there by Abascal and the legislative staff. This second negotiation also took five days. When we were near agreement, the negotiations came apart over our refusal to include an annual cost of living increase for AFDC which had not been part of the original agreement. Beilenson blew up, stormed out, and did not come out of his office for several days. Although his name was the lead author on the final welfare reform bill, he doggedly opposed its implementation.

Meese met with McCarthy and eventually agreed to the annual cost of living increase as the price for reform. The original agreement was intact, with the addition of the cost of living adjustments (COLAs), which had been opposed most vehemently by me. COLAs should be considered each year in conjunction with other reforms to offset their cost, not etched in the stone of legislation. Democratic governor Jerry Brown regretted the COLAs and tried to eliminate them when he was governor, but they had been put there by his legislators. The COLAs were no problem for Ronald Reagan, since the reforms and our implementation of them kept the spending under control.

Through all of this, Ronald Reagan proved that he was a master negotiator. He also proved that to be successful the negotiator must know his subject. Reagan knew the elements of welfare reform.

The Welfare Reform Act, consisting of over eighty-four elements and many subelements, was signed into law as an emergency measure on August 13, 1971. When Governor Reagan signed the bill in his office, I was in Denver addressing a previously scheduled special session of the Colorado legislature and missed the ceremonial signing. Reagan sent Ed Meese, Jim Hall, and others to meet me on his behalf at the airport on my return that night. We celebrated the victory with champagne.

The bill took effect on October 1, 1971.

3

What Had Always Gone Up—Finally Comes Down

The Welfare Reform Act was subjected to court attacks, including those by its nominal author, Mr. Moretti, and other legislative negotiators who did not realize the extent to which they were agreeing to true welfare reform until after the bill had been enacted. At that point, they found themselves on the receiving end of extreme heat and criticism from their supporters in social workers' unions, welfare rights organizations, and similarly minded factions.

Some analysts who tried to attribute much of the decline of California's welfare rolls to economic conditions pointed out that the decline in the state's welfare rolls started months before the California Welfare Reform Act (CWRA) became effective. It is true that welfare rolls started dropping in early 1971 and the CWRA was not effective until October 1971. However, the point that is missed is that the legislation only constituted a part of the "welfare reform program." The "program" actually began in January 1971, with the implementation of numerous administrative and regulatory reforms aimed at stopping the explosive growth of the rolls.

As 1971 began, the welfare rolls were growing at the rate of approximately 40,000 persons per month. Indeed, the rolls continued their upward climb through March 1971. Then in April, about two months after we issued our initial administrative and regulatory reforms, AFDC rolls appeared to drop by about 25,000 persons, after having risen each month for many years. I thought that a county or two must have been missed in the count, so I did not announce the drop. Then the rolls dropped again in May. This time, we announced the two-month drop. By the time November closed, the rolls had been reduced by 180,000 from the figure set at our starting point in January.[1]

In December, the rolls increased temporarily because of a California Supreme Court decision that was later reversed by the U.S. Supreme Court. That month, the governor noted that we had brought welfare under control in California and that we expected the welfare situation to stabilize.

But in January 1972, the rolls dropped again, shortly after the Welfare Reform Act became fully operative. With the exception of December 1971, the AFDC and general assistance rolls declined each and every month

1. California Department of Social Welfare, "Public Assistance Case Loads and Expenditures." March 1971–November 1971.

for two years after we announced the initial drop. All of our expectations for welfare reform were exceeded.

By the end of 1972, over 300,000 fewer persons were on the rolls since the high of March 1971, and we had avoided the growth of 500,000 additional persons predicted by the legislative analyst, A. Alan Post. Post had made his predictions before the legislature at budget sessions in 1971, where his office challenged our estimates.

The initial drop in the rolls was caused by our administrative and regulatory changes, instituted in the first few months of 1971, but the continuing drop was ensured by the Welfare Reform Act, which became operative in October. The Welfare Reform Act included benefit increases for truly needy families, just as Governor Reagan had promised. Reagan had first proposed benefit increases to truly needy families, which would be paid for in reform savings. But our opponents did not believe that we would achieve the savings. Consequently, they claimed there would be no benefit increase. But we achieved our savings by June 1972, and I ordered a 26 percent across-the-board increase for June 1.

One month later, a federal court unnecessarily echoed my across-the-board increase with an across-the-board order of its own. The federal Ninth Circuit Court of Appeals later reversed district court judge Zirpoli's order in a scathing decision. Illegal or not, the district court order was superfluous. We had increased benefits voluntarily, just as we had announced we would do.

Illogical Opponents

The success of Governor Reagan's welfare reform program served to embarrass those who opposed it and those who supported the proposed federal redistribution scheme known as the Family Assistance Plan, so there was a concerted effort by many to discredit the effects of the governor's reforms.

First, detractors claimed that the drop in welfare in California was the result of a drop in the unemployment rate and the birth rate. The facts show otherwise.

Over the ten years preceding welfare reform in California, the welfare rolls—particularly the unemployed father rolls—climbed every year. The increases were unrelenting. However, in no less than six of those ten years, the unemployment rate dropped!

In contrast, during the administrative reforms of 1971, the welfare rolls fell for several months, long before the first measurable drop in the unemployment rate. And after the legislature took action, despite the many attempts to water down or diminish legislative reforms, the act was a real success, even according to some of its critics.[2]

Then there were the demographic arguments. Even though there had been a gradual reduction in the birth rate, it was hard to believe that anyone could seriously claim that the birth rate slowed so suddenly as to cause welfare rolls that had been growing at the rate of 40,000 to 50,000 a month to reverse themselves abruptly in March 1971, and thereafter continue to go down.

---

2. Frank Levy, *Studies in American Politics and Public Policy*, 4th edition (Cambridge, MA: The M.I.T. Press, 1978), chapter 14.

We did notice, however, a rather sharp reduction in the average number of children per case. This, coincidentally, occurred with the completion of the eligibility audit program. The California welfare recipient now knew that there was a very good chance that the number of children he reported would be checked and audited. Moreover, the eligibility worker now knew that his or her work would be audited. The task force had found during its study that a major form of fraud and abuse was to overreport the number of children in a family, in order to obtain a higher grant.

Third, some detractors claimed that the liberal 1967 California abortion law contributed heavily to the reduction in the AFDC rolls. One legislator who made this argument was the author of the abortion act, who, while it was under consideration, argued that it would not significantly increase the number of abortions in California—it would merely make them safer. He may have been correct at the time, because the California birth rate showed no significant change during the year following the abortion act. In fact, just as in the case of unemployment rates in the years preceding the welfare reforms, the birth rate in California and the rest of the nation dropped virtually every year—while each year the family welfare rolls continued to grow. This was one of the anomalies of the welfare system before the 1971–73 reforms. There was no effective correlation between the economy, employment, birth rates, and the growth of the welfare rolls. Despite a growing economy and declining birth rates, welfare rolls grew out of control.

Beyond California

Those who tried to negate California's success in reversing the explosive growth of its welfare rolls should have pondered the experiences of other large industrial states where similar conditions existed and where the rolls continued to increase until California-style reforms were instituted. When Governor Nelson A. Rockefeller did so in 1972 and 1973, there followed the first annual drop of the number of persons on welfare in New York since 1960. Indeed, it was the largest drop since World War II.[3]

I met with Governor Rockefeller as well as members of his staff on several occasions in 1971 and 1972 to brief them and to provide details of elements of the California welfare reforms of that period. In 1975, during my tenure as U.S. Commissioner of Welfare, at a meeting with then–Vice President Rockefeller, he stated that the decline in New York's rolls was largely the result of reforms patterned after the California model.

With the welfare rolls dropping in the two largest states in 1972 and 1973, some superficial observers concluded that the nation's rolls were "saturated" and "leveling off." In fact, the reductions were the fruit of stringent reforms, fashioned and fought for by two governors, Reagan in 1971 and Rockefeller a year later.

3. New York State Department of Social Services, *1973 Annual Report,* Legislative Document (1974) No. 93, Publication No. 1016 (474), April 10, 1974.

Welfare with a Purpose

It is impossible to determine to what extent individual elements of the 1971–73 California Welfare Reform Program, either administrative or legislative, contributed to its success. Many of the reforms were overlapping and interrelated. All combined to form a genuine comprehensive program.

The only way to keep score is to look at the actual caseloads, as opposed to what they were projected to be, and to observe the increased benefits to the truly needy remaining on the rolls.

From the time the administrative reforms began to take effect in March 1971, until the close of the Reagan administration in late 1974, there were over 850,000 fewer persons on family welfare and general assistance programs than were projected by legislative and other experts prior to the 1971 reforms. There was an absolute reduction of AFDC and general assistance rolls by more than 300,000 persons. Despite massive benefit increases to the needy aged, blind, disabled, and families, total welfare expenditures *dropped* in fiscal year 1972–73 for the first time. Benefit levels to families increased by over 43 percent, and cost-of-living and standard-of-living increases to the aged, blind, and disabled were financed.

Nearly nine years later, in January 1980, there were still nearly 300,000 fewer persons on AFDC and general assistance in California than in March 1971, and state supplemental benefits to the federal Supplemental Security Income program for the aged, blind, and disabled were virtually the highest in the nation. California's AFDC error rates were the lowest of any major industrial state.

California demonstrated that, even under the old welfare system, a state did have the flexibility to provide significant reforms if it was willing to take on the task and not merely give up and shift the burden to the federal level. With more freedom from federal regulation, the states could do even more for the taxpayer and the needy.

The unifying philosophy of the welfare reform was summed up by Governor Reagan in his 1972 presentation to the Senate Finance Committee:

> Welfare needs a purpose—to provide for the needy, of course—but more than that to salvage their own fellow citizens to make them self-sustaining and, as quickly as possible, to make them independent of welfare. There has been something terribly wrong with a program that grows ever larger even when prosperity for everyone else is increasing. We should measure welfare successes by how many people leave welfare, not by how many are added.

It is easy to forget the realities of that time and the sequences of events that took place from the fall of 1970 through early 1973, the key time of the California welfare reform program. Political considerations, bruised egos, and other factors tended to skew many interpretations and evaluations of the project's effectiveness. But eventually, the consensus was that the 1971–73 reforms were effective. Even Governor Reagan's successor, Governor Jerry Brown, agreed that the program worked amazingly well.[4] He indicated to me on several occasions in 1975, when I was U. S. Commissioner of Welfare, that he intended to continue the Reagan reforms.

4. Carl Ingram, UPI wire service, Sacramento, CA, August 10, 1975.

4

The Essential Elements of Redistribution

Welfare reform—that's what Domestic Advisor Joe Califano labeled a comprehensive guaranteed income program that he presented to President Lyndon B. Johnson in the mid-1960s. Johnson rejected it. It was too big and too liberal.[1]

But when Richard Nixon became president, he bought into substantially the same plan. Through the efforts of his domestic advisor Daniel Patrick Moynihan and others, it was sold with conservative rhetoric: It

---

1. The history relating to the Johnson years and the origins of the first Nixon Family Assistance Plan was derived by me principally from the book *Nixon's Good Deed: Welfare Reform* by Vincent J. and Vee Burke (New York: Columbia University Press, 1974). All other material is from my personal experiences.

would provide cash benefits to intact families to hold the families together and strengthen work incentives by letting families earn more without losing welfare benefits. The cash benefits plan was a cover for a move toward universal eligibility, and the work incentives plan was a cover for adding millions of workers to the income redistribution system. Nixon and many conservatives bought these arguments. The proposal was known as the Family Assistance Plan, or FAP.

FAP would be an efficient incomc rcdistribution system. An efficient system for redistributing income needs three features to be workable: universal eligibility, a national number, and benefits in the form of cash. I call it the "three-legged stool." Universal eligibility means that everyone is eligible, not just widows and orphans, the disabled, etc. The only test is income and assets. A national number means that a minimum benefit level or other national benefit level is determined by Congress. Benefits must be in the form of cash because people have a limited capacity to consume food, clothing, and housing, but an unlimited capacity to move up the benefit and eligibility levels, making millions of Americans eligible with each move.

As Senator Russell Long once told me, "Every two years one fellow will say, 'I'll raise you one thousand dollars,' and the other fellow will say, 'I will see this one thousand and raise you two.'"

Incremental efforts to attain the "three-legged stool" took such forms as making more groups (for example, intact working families) eligible for Aid to Families with Dependent Children (AFDC) and defining "unemployed" in terms of the amount of monthly income earned rather than the number of hours worked. Other examples of incremental change are a national minimum benefit level in AFDC and a cash-out of the Food Stamp Program. The Food Stamp Program already has two of the three legs in place: universal eligibility and benefit levels set by Congress. If benefits were to be given in cash instead of food stamps, the last leg would be in place, and off we would go to efficient income redistribution (which is why it is imperative to block-grant these two federal programs to the states, and end their entitlement nature).

Like Califano's plan, the FAP proposal promised "a single equitable system," "uniform national standards," "simplification of eligibility requirements," and other panaceas pushed by the welfare establishment. Yet these proposals were aimed not at welfare reforms based on need, but at an efficient system for the redistribution of income. This was not the solution to the welfare problem.

The plan sailed through the House of Representatives with bipartisan support, but it stalled in Senator Long's Finance Committee when Health, Education, and Welfare secretary Finch could not respond to the tough questions asked.

FAP was reintroduced in 1971 as House Resolution 1, with Ways and Means chairman Wilbur Mills as sponsor. Again it sailed through the House. On February 1, 1972, Governor Reagan went before Senator Russell Long's Finance Committee to testify against the bill. (Reagan's testimony is reprinted in this book's appendix.)

The evening before Reagan's testimony, I was sitting next to him on the airplane. He pointed out to me the grain elevators throughout the Midwest, each of which was the focus of a town. Each town was there as a central point for farmers to take their grain to market. Life in that area revolved around on the town. There were thousands of such towns in middle America, he told me, and they had the same conservative values that he had.

I mentioned to him that this was my wedding anniversary. He was dismayed that I would be away from home on such an occasion, and asked why hadn't I told him sooner. My reply was that he might not have let me go if I had. He answered, "Maybe, maybe not."

The next day, as we got out of the car at the Dirksen Senate office building, staffers gathered along the hallways to see Ronald Reagan. At the Finance Committee hearing, all the Democrats were in attendance, most of them eager to show up this Hollywood actor.

I sat at the witness table with the governor. Through his prepared testimony, we provided a long list of legislative changes—opposed by the income redistribution establishment—that would make true welfare reform possible at the state level. Reagan labeled FAP a national guaranteed-income plan. He recommended state solutions as an alternative, based on his successful California welfare reforms. The governor held forth for over two hours, answering every question right to the point. One by one, the liberal Democratic senators peeled off and left the room. I heard one whisper to his seatmate as he left, "This guy is too good for me."

After hearing Reagan's testimony, Chairman Long told the governor that he was the best governmental witness the committee had heard. Long then asked him privately if he could "borrow" me to prepare the recommended legislation. The governor readily agreed, and for the next year I made trips to Washington about once a month to supply Senator Long with legislation that he would attach to the next veto-proof bill to pass through his committee to final passage.

After I became U.S. Commissioner of Welfare in Nixon's second term, with the consent of HEW secretary Caspar Weinberger I continued my working relationship with Chairman Long. Then, during Gerald Ford's administration, with Governor Reagan's help, I beat back at the presidential level one more attempt at a guaranteed-income program emanating from HEW.

Carter Tries Welfare Reform

But before long, Joe Califano was back. President Jimmy Carter appointed him to the critical position of secretary of HEW. Carter had announced that his welfare reform program would entail a list of elements. The first was Carter's specific requirement: that the reform could cost no more than what was being spent on the system at that time. This would leave no room for the Califano-led redistributionists to operate, so Califano began holding hearings around the country on Carter's list of welfare reform elements. I believed that the purpose of those hearings was to build political support for a costly income redistribution scheme labeled "welfare reform," and to overcome Carter's conservative requirement that the reform could have no increase in cost.

One Saturday morning in August 1977, after Congress had adjourned for its August recess, Carter was home in Plains, Georgia. There he announced his welfare reform plan, called "Better Jobs and Income." I thought that Carter was lukewarm toward the plan, because it admittedly would cost over $2 billion dollars more than was currently being spent, thus violating his promise.

I worked all day Saturday and through the night analyzing the lengthy bill, gleaning several potential horror stories. I relayed those scenarios to Ken Tomlinson, then senior editor (and later editor in chief) of *Reader's Digest*. All day and night, Ken wrote draft press releases based on my analyses. Then the American Conservative Union sent Ken's press releases to the homes of conservative congressmen and senators across the country. They, in turn, issued the releases in specific attacks on the Carter plan.

As predicted, the Carter plan was generally the same as the Califano plan rejected by Johnson and accepted by Nixon. It was a comprehensive plan for an income redistribution system containing the three key elements I outlined earlier—universality, simplicity, and uniformity. In my immediate analysis, I estimated that the plan would cost initially over $20 billion dollars more than the current system. This figure was confirmed, eventually, by the Congressional Budget Office.

A special joint subcommittee of three House committees was created, chaired by Congressman James Corman, to hold hearings on the bill. During the hearings, I prepared analyses and questions for the Republican members. But the Carter plan failed to get a hearing from any of the substantive committees. A partisan vote of the special joint subcommittee killed the bill.

Then, in December 1977, I was contacted by Senator

Long. He was concerned about a new "Businessmen's Committee for the Federalization of Welfare." The committee was headquartered in New York City and consisted of CEOs of many Fortune 500 companies, most of which were headquartered in the northeast. He wanted me to conduct a campaign to educate these key businessmen and turn them around on this issue. He said he would make the initial contacts with key committee members. I was to explain to these business leaders how federalization of welfare was a cover phrase for a system for effective income redistribution.

I began with David Rockefeller, and I was successful. Rockefeller, in turn, had me brief leaders of the Business Roundtable, which in turn created a committee on the subject. It took over two years of discussion and persuasion against heavy opposition, but we succeeded in at least neutralizing the roundtable.[2]

Those who were dedicated to income redistribution fell into two categories: comprehensive reformers and incrementalists. At the start of a new administration, the comprehensive crowd usually wins out. A big, costly welfare reform plan is put forward, and because of its high cost and size, it is easier to defeat. This is what Carter first attempted in 1977. (In Nixon's case they tried the comprehensive plan twice because they had the support of the House Democratic leadership. In my opinion, Nixon's second effort would have succeeded were it not for Russell Long and Ronald Reagan.)

---

2. Through the three years of working with the big business community and countering the second Carter welfare reform effort of 1979 with Senator Long, my efforts were financed by my acting as a consultant to nine major companies recruited by Senator Long.

I worried most about Carter's second "incremental" reform effort, which was sold as a simple fix-it plan that would cost relatively little. But it contained the three key elements for a efficient system of income redistribution: universal eligibility based on income, not family composition; a national minimum benefit; and a cash system including, if possible, a cash-out of food stamps. This plan was dangerous because it attracted moderate Republicans and some social conservatives who fell for it because it included benefits for intact working families–even though the massive Seattle-Denver and New Jersey income maintenance experiments of the 1970s showed that welfare to intact working families caused a *greater* break-up of those families than if they received *no* welfare benefits. (The income redistribution crowd who instituted the experiments to prove their case were appalled at the results and have tried to quash or discredit them ever since.)

Carter Tries Again

Carter emphasized that his new plan would be "administered" at the state rather than at the federal level. The feds would make the rules. The states were merely clerks. But we were ready for them because of Russell Long's and my efforts in 1978.

I had written two similar "block grant" bills, one for the House and one for the Senate. Each contained a provision for workfare. These bills would be *our* incremental effort to move welfare decision-making to the states. While we did not expect them to pass, they gave a political haven to Republicans and moderate Democrats who were beguiled by the Carter effort. We got the total support of Ways and Means Committee Republicans and Democrat Jim Jones. All House Republicans and many House Democrats voted for our bill, H.R. 4460. It failed by about five votes, but it succeeded in making the Carter bill a partisan rather than a bipartisan effort. The Carter bill was passed by a small majority in the House. In the Senate, the senior Democrats and the senior Republicans on the Finance Committee, including Chairman Long and ranking Republican Bob Dole, were the initial sponsors of our bill, S. 1382. The House-passed Carter welfare bill received no hearing before the full Finance Committee, and it died there. We did not intend to move our bill, because a hostile House would have emasculated it. It had served its purpose as a bipartisan haven for moderate Democrats and Republicans.

5

Rules for Reform

Welfare reform is inherently complicated. It involves an infinite number of variables. There is no all-inclusive cause or simple remedy for the welfare problem.

The need for assistance may arise for a variety of reasons: because of a death in the family, divorce, unemployment, or disability; the need for job training, child care, education, or medical treatment. Or it may arise because of a lack of motivation, sloth, greed, or incarceration. For an individual or a family, it may include any number or combination of these conditions, or none of them. Conditions may be permanent or of short duration, long duration, intermittent, or nonexistent. When a true need exists, aid must be prompt. And when need ends, aid must be ended instantly. Needs and eligibility should be verified on a regular or continuing basis to ensure the accuracy of eligibility and benefits.

No federally developed or administered system can provide for all variables, properly diagnose the cause of need and dependency, take steps to direct the necessary cure, and also assure adequate verification in each instance when benefits are sought or provided. A welfare system must therefore be designed and administered at the local or state level of government, in order to tailor the assistance to meet the temporary needs of the community's truly needy in a timely and accurate manner. In my opinion, an effective work requirement can be developed and run only at the local or state level.

What the Liberals Didn't Want to Hear

In fact, the massive Seattle-Denver income maintenance experiment had disproved the major contentions of those who supported the guaranteed family income plans of the Nixon and Carter administrations. This major experiment found that people work less when they are guaranteed a minimum income. It also found that families enrolled in guaranteed income programs are more likely to break up than families not enrolled in such programs.

Completed in the summer of 1979, the experiment was funded by the U.S. Department of Health, Education, and Welfare and involved the states of Washington and Colorado, SRI International, and Mathematica Policy Research. The experiment included

> over 5,000 people testing 11 variations of the negative income tax (guaranteed income), some for a 3–7-year period and some for a 5-year period, with 40 percent of the participants acting as a control group. . . . This experiment provides the best evidence to date on the effect of a negative income tax on work effort and is the most extensive study ever attempted on this issue. Those in the welfare establishment who called for the study expected to find that individuals would work more if allowed to keep a greater portion of their welfare benefit. On the contrary, the experiment showed that families reduced their work effort. . . .

The experiment also revealed unexpected findings in the area of families with guaranteed income breaking up. While welfare proponents argued that "current welfare programs in which benefits are cut off if the father is living with the family have been a major incentive for family breakup," the study found a higher rate of marital collapse for families with guaranteed income. The results showed that when families received guaranteed income at 90 percent of the poverty level, there was a 43 percent increase in black family dissolution and a 63 percent increase in white family dissolution. At 125 percent of the poverty level, the black family dissolution rate showed a 73 percent increase while for white families dissolution increased at a rate of 40 percent.[1]

1. "The Researchers Destroy Some Welfare Myths," Chamber of Commerce of the United States of America, Washington, D.C., 1979.

Efficient Redistribution

Let's revisit a concept that was touched on briefly in chapter 4. If I were asked, as a devil's advocate, to design an efficient system for the redistribution of the nation's income, I would agree that such a plan must be universal, simple, and uniform. It must be an engine fueled by the political dynamics of a representative democracy. This system would really require only three main characteristics:

1. ***Universal eligibility.*** All individuals and families with income below an established minimum would be eligible for the program. Categorical tests for eligibility on the basis of age, blindness, disability, widow or orphan status, unemployment, etc., would be jettisoned.
2. ***Benefit levels set by Congress.*** Benefits would be established for the nation as a whole. At present, welfare benefit levels (except for food stamps) are set by the states.
3. ***Cash benefits.*** Benefits would be in the form of cash, because people have a limited capacity to consume food, clothing, or housing but an unlimited capacity to consume cash.

Two other elements would be useful *but not necessary*. One would be that the system be administered entirely by a federal agency, and the other that there be no work requirement. A work requirement implies a *quid pro quo,* and would be replaced by "work incentives," a euphemism which really means "no work requirement."

The system could work with "state administration" as long as the federal government set all standards and rules, reducing the states to the status of clerks.

Consider what would happen next, if such an income redistribution mechanism were set in place. The political dynamics of representative democracy would accelerate the redistribution process. Irresistible pressures would build on Congress to increase the centrally set benefit levels. Millions of additional persons would receive cash benefits. More pressure then would build for more benefits from a greater number of constituents. Additional benefits would be added, and on and on, until most Americans would be receiving cash benefits. Eventually, the nation's economic system would collapse.

Traditionally, business people, professionals, fiscal moderates, and conservatives have steered clear of welfare matters. Consequently, welfare, a functional area, has been dominated by well-meaning persons who are advocates of the poor, and by socialists. The advocates of the poor see redistribution of income as a correction of an inequity; socialists see the welfare system as a means of realizing their goals for achieving a different economic system. Thus, welfare-reform alternatives have been limited by this welfare establishment to two approaches—"comprehensive" and "incremental" reform.

Comprehensive Reform

"Comprehensive" reform would install in one move

a federally administered, congressionally set cash assistance program, with universal eligibility based on income only—all of the characteristics of an efficient system for redistributing income. The 1977 Carter-Califano-Corman welfare reform plan, the negative income tax, and the ill-fated McGovern welfare proposal of 1972 are all examples of such "comprehensive" reform.

The first year cost of the sweeping 1977 Carter-Califano-Corman bill over the expense of the existing welfare system was estimated by the Congressional Budget Office (CBO) to exceed $21 billion. Other experts' figures ranged higher; Senator Russell Long estimated a cost of at least $60 billion shortly after the first year.[2] Even the low estimate meant a doubling of the cost of the system. Worse, 60 million people would be eligible for direct, federally administered cash benefits in the first year, compared to 21 million in 1980.

However, many influential members of the welfare establishment admitted that although "comprehensive" reform had "desirable" goals, it was politically impractical. The costs were high and the effects were obvious, as the 1977 CBO report demonstrated; therefore, time would be lost while an alerted Congress and public debated the proposal. Instead, these members of the welfare establishment proposed "incremental" welfare reform.

---

2. Adam Clymer, "Carter Welfare Bid Is Criticized by Long: Senate Finance Committee Chief Assails Cost and Predicts an Increase in Dependency," the *New York Times*, September 15, 1977.

Incremental Reform

When the Carter administration's 1977 comprehensive reform failed to get a hearing before the House Ways and Means Committee because of its obvious high cost and coverage, "incremental" welfare reform became the fall-back position of the welfare establishment.

Shortly before Congress adjourned in 1978, Senator Edward Kennedy (D-MA) introduced the classic "incremental" welfare reform bill. It was backed by the Carter administration.[3]

On June 5, 1979, the Carter administration introduced what became H.R. 4904, sponsored by congressmen James Corman (D-CA) and Al Ullman (D-OR), and others.[4]

A companion bill, S. 1290, was introduced in the Senate.[5] Referred to as the Carter-Kennedy-Corman bill, it was very similar to the Kennedy incremental welfare reform bill of late 1978. Its sponsors attempted to give the impression that this piece of legislation had

---

3. S. 3498, introduced September 14, 1978, would have provided a national minimum benefit for AFDC, mandated the AFDC Unemployed Parent Program for states that did not provide such assistance, eliminated the one-hundred-hour requirement for the AFDC Unemployed Parent programs, and made other centralizing changes in the welfare system.
4. The administration's bill was introduced on June 5, 1979, as H.R. 4321 and referred to the House Ways and Means Committee, where it was amended and renumbered H.R. 4904.
5. S. 1290, introduced June 6, 1979, was sponsored by senators Edward Kennedy (D-MA), Daniel P. Moynihan (D-NY), Harrison A. Williams Jr. (D-NJ), Howard Baker (R-TN), Henry Bellmon (R-OK), John Danforth (R-MO) Mark Hatfield (R-OR), and others.

a relatively low annual cost. They especially did not want to see the bill labeled as "guaranteed income," but that is exactly what it was. It contained the same major elements as the family assistance plans of 1969 and 1971, and of the Carter administration's welfare reform plan of 1977. By establishing a national minimum-benefit level for Aid to Families with Dependent Children (AFDC), mandating that all states include an AFDC program for intact families with "unemployed" breadwinners, and changing the definition of "unemployed" to income instead of hours worked, all the key ingredients necessary for a national guaranteed income for families were present. In addition, by federalizing and liberalizing the assets test and the definition and treatment of income, the administration's program reduced the states' role to that of clerks instead of partners. The so-called work requirement was even less stringent than in the existing unworkable system. If this proposal had been established, the political dynamics described earlier would be set in motion with pressures for increased benefit levels eventually adding millions of persons to the welfare rolls.

What Is the Answer?

Well then, what *was* the solution to the problem of providing help to those who really needed it?

True welfare reform lay in halting the movement toward federalization. Let the federal government make block grants to the states from the funds spent on family assistance, food stamps, and social services, and let the states design their own welfare systems. With federal regulations eliminated, the states would be able to provide relief to the taxpayer and, at the same time, would increase benefits to those who were truly in need. Eventually, the federal block grants could be supplanted by state funding if the federal government would return some of its taxing authority to the states.

Some people felt that state and local governments could not handle the welfare problem. Indeed, some believed that it was the fault of the states that there was such a welfare mess. However, this was not the case. Experience shows that state and local governments were able to reduce caseloads, costs, and error rates in the programs over which they had control. At the same time, many increased benefit levels.

In early 1973, I was appointed U.S. Commissioner of Welfare with a mandate from HEW secretary Caspar Weinberger to "help governors initiate their own welfare reforms similar to . . . Governor Reagan's in California."[6]

Largely as a result of implementing such reforms, after twenty years of unbroken growth, the number of persons receiving AFDC in the U.S. declined in calendar year 1973 and fiscal year 1974, and declined or remained stable after that. State action resulted in a reduction in error rates. The success of Title IV-D, the 1974 national child-support enforcement program,

---

6. I resigned from this post on August 13, 1975, and recommended that the job be abolished as a "symbolic gesture that welfare is a basic and primary responsibility of the states." I also said that abolishing the job "would be an important first step in reducing the size of the unnecessarily large federal welfare bureaucracy."

closely patterned after California's successful reforms and sponsored by Senator Long, surpassed the predictions of its most ardent supporters. Much of this success was in spite of active opposition by those people in HEW and elsewhere who continued to press for a national guaranteed income.

The one-man, one-vote decision of the U.S. Supreme Court[7] increased representation for urban areas in the states, and the Voting Rights Act of 1965 and the Civil Rights Act of 1974 enfranchised the black poor. As a result, benefits were increased in previously low-benefit states. Mississippi, for example, increased its benefits to a family of four by 100 percent in July 1978. Benjamin L. Hooks, executive director of the National Association for the Advancement of Colored People (NAACP), recognized this phenomenon in a statement before the National Governors' Association in February 1978. Hooks said: "Recently, we have come to the conclusion [that] there has been a change, and there has been a new sense of responsiveness" on the part of state governments to the needs of the black community.

The open-ended matching financing structure of the AFDC program, however, tended to minimize the incentive for states to make their programs more effective. The federal government assumed a large portion (50 to 80 percent) of state costs on a completely open-ended basis. The more states spent or wasted, the more federal money came in. On the other hand, when states cut down on spending by eliminating waste or moving people from welfare to employment, they lost federal

7. *Reynolds v. Sims* 377 U.S. 533 (1964)

matching funds. This system rewarded waste and penalized economical management. Proposals to provide fiscal relief to states by way of increased matching would only worsen this situation.

By using a block-grant funding approach, instead of a matching approach, the incentive could be reversed. The amount of the grant could be established at the level required to replace federal funding with whatever additional amount for fiscal relief would be found necessary. That grant level—once established for a state and indexed for inflation, population changes, and unusually high unemployment—would remain in place without regard to increases or decreases in the state's caseload. This would give each state the strongest possible incentive to improve the operation and structure of its program. If an ineligible person were kept off the rolls, or an eligible person given a job, the full amount saved would be available to the state to use for increasing the grants to eligible persons, or for whatever purpose the state found appropriate.

The Family Welfare Improvement Act (S. 1382) was introduced in the Senate on June 20, 1979, by senators Russell Long and Bob Dole, and others.[8] Its companion bill, H.R. 4460, was introduced in the House on June 14, 1979, by congressmen Barber Conable (R-NY) and John Rousselot (R-CA), and others.[9] The bill of-

---

8. S. 1382 was sponsored initially by senators Russell Long (D-LA), Bob Dole (R-KS), Herman Talmadge (D-GA), Bob Packwood (R-OR), Lloyd Bentsen (D-TX), Richard Schweiker (R-PA), and David Boren (D-OK).

9. H.R. 4460 was sponsored initially by congressmen Barber Conable (R-NY), John Rousselot (R-CA), Trent Lott (R-MS), James Jones (D-OK), Philip Crane (R-IL), Willis Gradison (R-

fered steps toward greater state innovation and control. This legislation would replace the present open-ended AFDC matching system with one of block grants, provide additional funds for fiscal relief and increase basic benefits in low-benefit states, and permit eight or ten demonstration states the complete freedom to design and implement their own welfare programs for families with children.

The goals of S. 1382 and H.R. 4460 were to:

- Limit the growth of expenditures for the open-ended federal family welfare program.
- Provide a strong incentive for the states to eliminate error, waste, and fraud in welfare programs and to reduce overall welfare spending.
- Provide all states with fiscal relief that could be used to reduce overall state welfare spending and to increase basic benefits for the truly needy.
- Encourage the states with the lowest per capita average income and lowest benefits to increase their basic family welfare benefit levels.
- Reverse the trend toward complete federalization of welfare by permitting eight or ten "demonstration states" to design and implement their own family welfare programs tailored to meet the individual needs of their states and their poor. Demonstration states would include a major industrial state, a ru-

---

OH), W. Henson Moore (R-LA), Robert Walker (R-PA), James Collins (R-TX), James Abdnor (R-SD), and Wayne Grisham (R-CA).

ral state, and others drawn by lot from states whose governors volunteered.

- Eliminate the need for a large federal bureaucracy to monitor the present open-ended federal matching system.
- Permit the states complete discretion to require work as a condition of eligibility for family welfare benefits.
- Reduce real federal spending for AFDC after 1986 by 2 percent per year to permit the federal budget to share the states' reductions in waste.

The next step would be to permit all other states to join the eight or ten demonstration states in being free of all federal direction in designing and administering their family welfare programs. Later, federal block grants could be replaced by the federal government relinquishing some of its taxing authority to the states.

By the autumn of 1979, two competing proposals were before Congress. They led in divergent directions. The Carter-Kennedy-Corman proposal cleared the House Ways and Means Committee on a partisan basis, opposed by all Republicans and three Democrats. The alternative block grant proposal, H.R. 4460, received the support of all committee Republicans and one Democrat, but was voted down by the Democratic majority. By a similar partisan vote, the Ways and Means Committee, the Rules Committee, and the House voted that the Carter-Kennedy-Corman bill be considered by the House with a "closed rule," precluding amendments or submittal of H.R. 4460 as a substitute bill.

H.R. 4460 earned the support of all Republicans on the Ways and Means Committee and the Republican Research Committee chaired by Congressman Trent Lott (R-MS), and its welfare reform task force chaired by Congressman Robert Walker (R-PA). On October 30, 1979, by a unanimous vote—including Chairman Bud Shuster (R-PA) and Minority Leader John Rhodes (R-AZ)—the House Republican Policy Committee voted to support H.R. 4460 as "an initiative that provides true welfare reform" and to reject flatly the Carter-Kennedy-Corman proposal.

On November 7, 1979, after two hours of debate in the House, the Democratic leadership beat back a motion by the Republicans to send the administration bill back to committee and to provide for state-imposed work requirements.

The vote was close: 200–205. The subsequent vote on the Carter-Kennedy-Corman plan for further federalization of welfare and the establishment of a guaranteed income for families passed with an unimpressive margin, 222–184.[10]

The Carter-Kennedy-Corman proposal contained several minor sections devoted to "tightening" the present system, but the real issues were the historic establishment of a national guaranteed minimum benefit and further federalization.

According to Alan Ehrenhalt, reporting in the *Washington Star* on October 28, 1979:

10. For details on committee and House action see *Congressional Quarterly*, September 22, 1979, 2037, and November 10, 1979, 1534–36.

The welfare task force, Sacramento, January 19, 1971—left to right: Carl Williams, Jack Svahn, Ronald Zumbrun, Ronald Reagan, Bob Carleson, Chuck Hobbs, and Richard Malcom.

RONALD REAGAN
GOVERNOR

State of California
GOVERNOR'S OFFICE
SACRAMENTO 95814

March 22, 1971

Mr. Robert B. Carleson
124 Clunie Drive
Sacramento, California

Dear Bob:

Jim Hall has told me about the long hours and hard work you devoted to putting together the welfare and Medi-Cal reform package. As you know, I consider this to be the most important project undertaken by my Administration during our time in Sacramento.

Actually, we have only begun the struggle, and all of us will be called upon to respond in fullest measure again and again in the coming months. I know I can continue to call on you to give your best efforts to this cause.

Again, my thanks for all you are doing. Best regards.

Sincerely,

Ronald Reagan
RONALD REAGAN
Governor

P.S. I have enclosed for your personal library a copy of Meeting The Challenge with a personal note to you on page 6.

Jerry – The W.F. lines I left out go something like this.

– Our figures on potential savings if W.F. reform is enacted have been challenged & picked at on an almost daily basis. THOSE FIGS. are the result of a years study & research by a task force working with county W.F. officials through out the state.

With all due respect to the Legis. Analyst & to the legis. committees who have conducted hearings they cannot possibly have the background info. upon which to base valid estimates. I have full confidence in our projections – in fact WE HAVE BEEN SO CAREFUL WE probably HAVE underestimated the REAL savings THAT can actually BE achieved.

This note from Ronald Reagan was to a staffer about an addition to Reagan's address on welfare reform at the Los Angeles Town Hall on June 23, 1971. He gave this speech after the state legislature denied him the privilege of addressing a joint session. As a result of the legislature's shortsightedness, Reagan received statewide television coverage, which launched the battle for welfare reform.

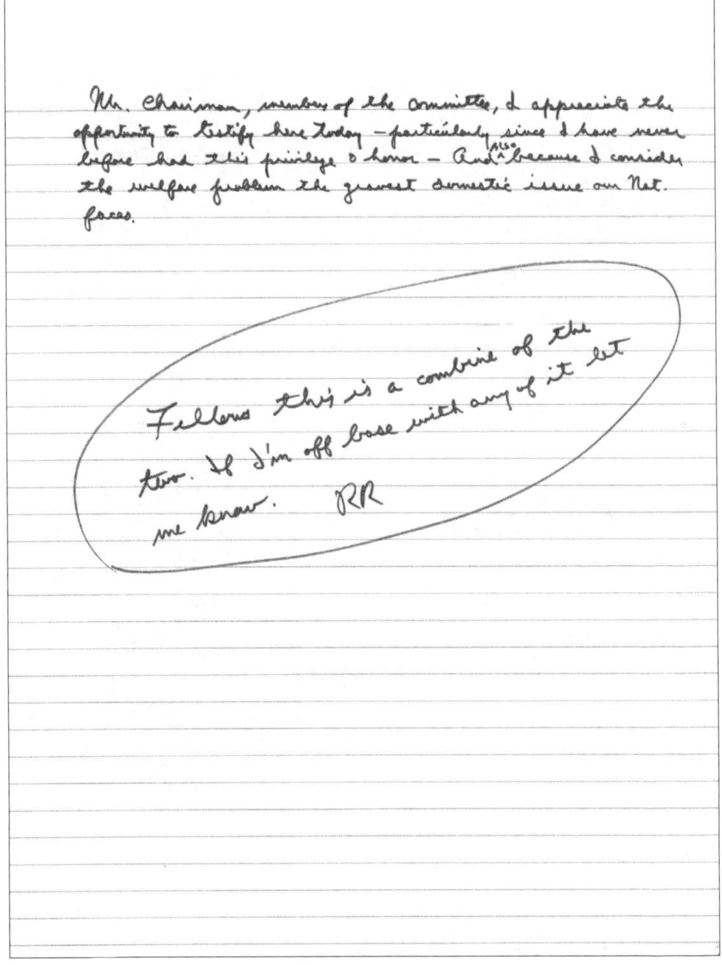

Mr. Chairman, members of the committee, I appreciate the opportunity to testify here today — particularly since I have never before had this privilege & honor — And also because I consider the welfare problem the gravest domestic issue our Nat. faces.

Fellows this is a combine of the two. If I'm off base with any of it let me know. RR

Here and on the following pages: Ronald Reagan's edits to the draft of his testimony before the U.S. Senate Finance Committee on February 1, 1972. (The final text of that testimony is provided in the appendix, beginning on page 143.)

STATEMENT OF GOVERNOR REAGAN

Two years ago welfare was out of control nationally and California was no exception. At that time Hr 16311, and later HR 1, were presented as a solution to the problem. One of its authors responded publicly to critical questions by answering that "It's better than sitting on our hands and doing nothing."

I share the President's ~~Nixon's~~ desire to reform welfare and certainly share his belief there should be a restoration of the work ethic. However, ~~However, as you are~~ As you are aware, I have had some very serious reservations about ~~to~~ several of the approaches to welfare reform embodied in HR 1.

In August 1970 I presented to this Committee a statement regarding the version of HR 16311 which was pending before your Committee. Many of the provisions of that Bill to which I objected in my statement are in HR 1.

My remarks today will concentrate on 6 areas of major concern I have with HR 1 and with the need for federal action in achieving real welfare reform. I believe that:

1. Given broad authority to utilize administrative and policy discretion the states are better equipped than the federal government to administer effective welfare reforms.
2. A system of a guaranteed income, whatever it may be called, would not be an effective reform of welfare but would tend to create an even greater human problem.
3. A limit should be set on the gross income that a family would receive and still remain eligible for welfare benefits.
4. For all those who are employable, a requirement be adopted that work in the community be performed as a condition of eligibility for welfare benefits without additional compensation.

5. The greatest single problem in welfare today is the breakdown of family responsibility and strong provision should be made to insure maximum support from responsible absent parents.

6. A simplified system of pensions should be established for the needy aged, blind, and the totally and permanently disabled.

THE STATE'S ABILITY TO ADMINISTER WELFARE

In August of 1970 the size and cost of welfare had grown to a monster which was devouring many of California's programs and was failing to meet the needs of those who, through no fault of their own, have nowhere else to turn but to government for SUBSISTENCE ~~their minimum needs~~.

WE DIDN'T JUST BECOME AWARE OF THIS PROBLEM IN 1970 BUT OUR EARLIER EFFORTS TO DEAL WITH IT WEREN'T TOO SUCCESSFUL PERHAPS BECAUSE WE RELIED ~~We had relied in the past~~ on ~~the~~ professional welfare experts to propose SOLUTIONS AND ALL TOO OFTEN THEY WERE MORE FAMILIAR WITH WHAT THEY WERE SURE THEY COULDN'T DO. SO HOWEVER ~~solutions. As a result~~ the situation became worse instead of better.

FINALLY ~~In order~~ to avert a fiscal and human disaster, I asked several members of my administration, who had proved themselves in other state administrative posts, to form a task force and to devote ~~their~~ full time for AS LONG AS IT TOOK ~~several months~~ ~~to review and analyze the entire public assistance situation in California~~ TO SEE IF & HOW REAL ~~so that a real~~ reform of welfare could be developed and implemented. THEY EXPANDED THEIR ~~The~~ task force ~~was expanded~~ to include experienced attorneys ~~in the private as well as the public sector~~ and other management and fiscal experts from THE PRIVATE SECTOR ~~outside of government, in California. For over four months this task force~~ THESE MEN & WOMEN SERVED ON A VOLUNTEER BASIS FOR 4 MONTHS REVIEWING ~~reviewed the~~ federal laws, state laws, & federal and state regulations.

THEY interviewed over 700 people involved in administering welfare in California at all levels, and developed ~~many~~ proposals and ideas for a realistic and humane reform of welfare. BY ~~In~~ January of 1971 WE WERE READY TO SET OUR COURSE AND WE BEGAN BY NAMING ONE MEMBER OF THE TASK FORCE ~~I appointed a member of this task force to become the new~~ Director of Social Welfare for the State of California, HE IMMEDIATELY BEGAN ~~and directed that he commence~~ implementation of the administrative changes and translated the knowledge gained from the task FORCE ACTIVITY INTO A RESPONSIBLE PROGRAM OF W.F. REFORM.

In early March of 1971 ~~[illegible]~~ not quite a year ago we presented the legislature what we think was the most comprehensive proposal for W.F. reform ever attempted. All in all there were over 70 major points involving admin., regulatory & legislative changes.

We had already gone ahead in Jan. with those changes we could make administratively and we continued through the spring & summer while the legis. considered the statutory changes we'd asked for.

It should be pointed out that we weren't exactly exploring uncharted land. Our task force findings had led to the conclusion that the basic—original structure of the WF system was sound. It was based on a concept of aid to the needy aged, the blind & disabled & to children deprived of parental support. Able bodied adults were expected to support them selves, their children & their aged parents to the extent of their capabilities. The system was meant to be administered by the states & counties with the Fed. govt. sharing in the cost.

But we had also learned that almost from the start this basic structure had been undermined. Sometimes by Fed. or state law but more often by regulations State & Fed. Regulations drawn up within the Fed. agency administering W.F. many times reflected the philosophy of the permanent employees ~~[illegible]~~ rather than an interpretation of the law and thus legislative intent was distorted.

Back in Jan. when we began there were plenty of experts telling us no state could reform W.F.; that the statutory, regulatory and admin. ~~[illegible]~~ constraints were too many & too inflexible. Figures would indicate they were wrong.

Page 4

H.E.W. has just released the infor. That NATIONALLY W.F. & I believe medicaid combined are increasing in cost ~~nationally~~ at an annual rate of 27%. In Calif. we have budgeted for the new fiscal year a 9% increase – $\frac{1}{3}$ the Nat. figure. And that doesn't tell the full story of what has happened because of our reforms. We think we may be playing it too safe.

For several years up until last April Calif's case load increased more than 40,000 persons per month. This held true even when the ec. was booming & we had full employment. Our projections in April were that by this last Dec. we would have added another 495,000 to the rolls. Not only did we not do this but in Dec. we had 176,000 fewer WF recipients than we had in April. In that 9 mo. figure we have reduced spending, Fed. St. & local by more than $120,000,000 below what it would have been without the reform.

Because of these savings we have achieved one of our primary goals – we have been able to increase the grants to the truly needy. An A.F.D.C. family of 4 to cite an example receiving $221 ~~monthly~~ last Spring now receives $280 a month. A cost of living increase was granted in Dec. to the aged, blind & disabled. In our 72-73 budget I mentioned a moment ago we are asking for $338,000,000 less in Fed. St. & County funds than would have been necessary without the reforms.

Let me stress once again – the important thing is we didn't find any new magic formula. We simply over hauled the present structurally sound W.F. system. We insured adequate aid to the

We believe our program simply overhauled the present structurally sound system, insuring adequate aid to the aged, the blind, the disabled, and children who are deprived of parental support and reduced aid to the non-needy with realistic work incentives so that funds could be redirected to the truly needy. Our program requires support from employable, responsible parents by requiring that jobs be taken, if offered, and that if jobs are not available, work in the community be performed to earn the grant. Absent parents are indebted to the county for aid rendered to their families with a provision for wage attachments and property liens, if necessary. But maybe most important is that the California plan retains most of the administration and responsibility for welfare at the level closest to those who benefit and those who pay the bill.

Members of our task force found that with provision for reasonable administrative discretion combined with fiscal responsibility and discipline the most effective administrative efforts in California were those carried on in the medium and smaller sized counties. We retained the concept of state supervision and county administration of welfare on a partnership basis. For smaller states, state administration may be desirable, but we see a fiscal and administrative disaster if the administration of the welfare system is centralized here in Washington, as proposed in HR 1. As you've already heard HEW claims H.R. 1 would save Calif. $234,000,000 — it would increase our costs by $900,000,000.

In spite of our reforms many of the greatest loopholes which permit abuse and inhibit effective state action and which have led to a loss of public confidence remain in federal law and federal regulation — mainly regulation.

We are presently being challenged in court on nine of our proposed changes on the grounds that we are in violation of Fed. law. We believe we are not in violation of Congressional intent before it was re-interpreted in regulations.

NO GUARANTEED INCOME

Page 6

TO GET BACK TO THE MATTER OF H.R. 1 I RESPECTFULLY URGE THIS COMMITTEE TO ELIM. THE PROPOSAL TO PROVIDE W.F. BENEFITS TO INTACT FAMILIES WITH EMPLOYED FATHERS. I AM NOT UNAWARE OF NOR INSENSITIVE TO THE PLIGHT OF THE LOW EARNER BUT I BELIEVE RELIEF TO THOSE FAMILIES CAN BE PROVIDED IN THE FORM OF

~~NO GUARANTEED INCOME~~

~~I would urge this committee to eliminate from HR 1 a new national program to that would provide welfare benefits to intact families with employed fathers.~~ I AM NOT UNAWARE OF THE PLIGHT OF THE LOW INCOME EARNER BUT I BELIEVE ~~I would urge that relief to these families be provided in the form of~~

Social Security and income tax exemptions. IT DOESN'T SEEM RIGHT TO REDUCE A MAN'S TAKE HOME PAY WITH TAXES & THEN SEND HIM A GOVT. DOLE WHICH ROBS HIM OF the feeling of accomplishment and dignity which comes from providing for his family by his own efforts. BY THE SAME TOKEN WE FEEL THE ABLE BODIED RECIPIENT SHOULD BE given the maximum opportunity to SUPPORT his family by DOING work in his community which will benefit the community AT THE SAME TIME IT DEVELOPS & maintains his ability to perform effectively in a regular job when it becomes AVAILABLE. WE DON'T SUGGEST THIS IN SOME PUNITIVE WAY NOR ARE WE ADVOCATING USELESS MAKE WORK CHORES. NOT ONLY WILL THE INDIVID. BENEFIT FROM PARTICIPATING IN USEFUL WORK IN RETURN FOR HIS WF. GRANT BUT THOSE WHO FOOT THE BILL WILL FEEL BETTER IF THEY SEE COMMUNITY SERVICES PERFORMED.

LIMIT ON GROSS INCOME AND WORK REQUIREMENT

I was pleased to see that the Talmadge Amendments were adopted by Congress and signed into law by the President. Most of the features of the Talmadge Amendments parallel very closely the separation of employables' portion of our California welfare reform program. However many of the so-called work incentives in the present system and in HR 1 as passed by the House of Representatives CONTINUE TO insure aid to the non-needy. AND Able-bodied adults are not required to work in the community to earn their grants.

We recommend that a realistic and absolute ceiling be placed on the income that a family may have and still be eligible for welfare. The experts tell us on one hand (AND I BELIEVE THEM) that all but a few welfare recipients would prefer to work if work or jobs were available YET on the other hand they tell us that we cannot expect someone to be willing to take a job or go to work if HIS WF grant IS significantly diminished. These expert opinions obviously are in conflict. I propose a combination of work incentives. An able-bodied recipient should be required to take a job if offered or perform

If I could anticipate a possible question concerning the usefulness of such a community work force let me mention one possibility. The L.A. school system reported last week that vandalism was costing that one city alone $50,000,000 a year. Night watchmen might change that.

community work if a job is not available, and in the case of a mother-headed family, reasonable work-related and child care expenses and a portion of her income could be exempted until she has stabilized her work situation. An absolute ceiling on the gross income a family may have and still be eligible for welfare should be set at 150% of the standard of need. The proposed limitation of work-related expenses contained in HR 1 should be retained.

FAMILY RESPONSIBILITY AND THE ABSENT FATHER —

Although we believe that the present grant sharing ratio between the state and the federal government should be retained, real fiscal relief can be given to the states, and at the same time help solve the problem of the breakdown in family responsibility caused by the lack of the absent father to provide for his family. We propose that the Federal Government adopt a plan similar to California's which would provide a support incentive fund which would permit the states or counties to retain 100% of the federal share of grants recovered through collections from absent fathers and through efforts of fraud control units.

PENSIONS FOR THE AGED, BLIND AND DISABLED —

I support the concept of a simplified system of pensions for the needy aged, blind, and totally and permanently disabled. Sums of money spent on costly and complicated eligibility and grant determination systems for these categories would be better spent in increasing benefits to these people, many of whom have provided adequately for themselves during their productive and working days but who have found that inflation has wiped out the fruits of these past accomplishments.

SUMMARY —

The effectiveness of the states and counties administration of welfare has come under heavy criticism and attack. PERHAPS IN A NUMBER OF INSTANCES this may be justified. However, it is almost impossible to hold a state accountable for effective administrative practices and policies under the present straight jacket of federal statutes, court interpretations, regulations, and abuses of administrative discretion. GIVE The states ~~should be given~~ the broadest authority to administer the system with PROPER goals and objectives and then ~~be held~~ HOLD US accountable ~~based on their~~ FOR OUR effectiveness in meeting these goals and objectives. Senator Curtis' approach in S-2037 to severely constrain the power of federal administrators and return authority to the states is definitely going in the right direction.

I am submitting at this time to you a more detailed listing of amendments that we would offer to HR 1 and urge your favorable consideration of them. They are the result of an actual reform program that is succeeding in Calif. They are not theory. I believe that we have demonstrated in California that a responsible approach to reform of the present welfare system is possible and that given tools, discretion, and adequate financial assistance, states and counties are in the best position to provide a welfare system patterned to meet the real needs of those in America who through no fault of their own have nowhere else to turn but to government. What Calif. has done – other states can do.

Welfare needs a purpose – to provide for the needy of course – but more than that; to salvage these our fellow citizens; to make them self sustaining and as quickly as possible independent of W.F. There has been some thing terribly wrong with a program that grows ever larger even when prosperity for every one else is increasing. We should measure welfares success by how many people leave WF not by how many more are added.

RBC/mc
1/26/72

Bob Carleson addresses New Hampshire legislators on January 21, 1974, as Governor Ronald Reagan and Governor Meldrin Thompson look on.

WELFARE RELATED MISSION AND GOALS OF THE DEPARTMENT OF HEALTH AND HUMAN SERVICES (HHS)

Mission of the Department

To reduce substantially the need for dependency on federal social, health and public assistance programs while, at the same time, to defend the integrity of Social Security insurance programs.

Major Goals Statement for Welfare Programs in HHS

1. Provide for an orderly and expeditious shift of authority and responsibility for the Aid to Families with Dependent Children (AFDC) Program to the states, through:

a) block grant funding
b) authority to the states to set all eligibility standards, benefit levels and work requirements without interference from the federal government
c) followed by a shift of taxing authority to replace block grants

2. Provide for an orderly and expeditious shift of authority and responsibility for the Medicaid program to the states, through:

a) block grant funding
b) authority to the states to set all eligibility standards and benefit levels, without interference from the federal government
c) followed by a shift of taxing authority to replace block grants

3. Eliminate loopholes and reduce fraud and abuse in all HHS programs, by adopting regulations and proposing legislation to close loopholes in eligibility requirements in aid programs (including AFDC and Medicaid) pending a shift to block grant status.

4. Transfer the food and nutrition programs from the Department of Agriculture to the Department of Health and Human Services.

5. Return the Medicare program to the Social Security Administration.

6. Consolidate AFDC, social services programs, Medicaid, food and nutrition programs and the policy function of the Supplemental Security Income program under an Assistant Secretary for Welfare.

7. Merge all social services programs into the Title XX block grant to the states.

As explained on pages 71–73, during the 1980–81 presidential transition, Bob Carleson created a decision-book for a major Reagan welfare reform. Here and on the following pages are excerpts from that decision-book, with Reagan's initials of approval. (The decision-book is available in its entirety at www.governmentistheproblem.us.)

8. Ensure that all social services are directed toward reducing dependency on public assistance.

9. Ensure that those persons who are able to work earn their public assistance benefits, with emphasis on state and local authority and action, <u>without any interference from the federal government</u>.

10. Develop an effective management system with emphasis on delegating authority to states to the maximum extent possible while maintaining the fiscal integrity of federal funding sources.

TRANSITION ACTION PAPER

BLOCK GRANTS FOR THE AID TO FAMILIES WITH DEPENDENT CHILDREN (AFDC) PROGRAM

Issue

Should the present open-ended matching system of financing the AFDC program be replaced with block grant funding with state discretion over all eligibility requirements, standards, benefit levels and work requirements?

Facts and Discussion

At present, the AFDC program is financed on an open-ended matching basis which encourages extravegance, waste and error. A capped block grant method of financing would reverse these state grant methods of financing, would reverse these state incentives. If states were given complete discretion over eligibility requirements, benefit levels, coverage and work requirements, they could best determine priorities for assistance to truly needy families and design systems which could be financed within the block grants. S.1328 (Long-Dole-Schweiker, et. al) and HR 4460 (Conable-Rousselot-Jones, et. al) introduced in the 96th Congress present a starting point for block granting AFDC. Consideration should be given, however, to reducing the proposed "fiscal relief" to the states in these bills in light of the present budget emergency. In addition, all states should be permitted complete freedom in designing their AFDC programs rather than the 8 or 10 states called for in the above legislation.

Recommendation

That legislation be submitted to "block grant" the AFDC program.

Regulation ☐

Legislation ☒

Approved ☒
Disapproved ☐
As Modified ☐

TRANSITION ACTION PAPER

COMPREHENSIVE NUTRITION BLOCK GRANT

Issue

Should the present array of federal nutrition programs be consolidated in one new block grant program administered by the states under broad federal guidelines?

Facts and Discussion

The US Department of Agriculture (USDA) nutrition programs (Food Stamps; School Lunch; Women, Infants and Children; Summer Feeding, etc.) are designed to improve the diet of Americans through federal food or financial assistance. The largest and most general in nature is the Food Stamp Program which currently reaches over 10 percent of the population. Other programs are targeted towards segments of the population which have been deemed to be of special nutritional importance, such as pregnant women and infants.

The nutrition programs are administered through state and local agencies according to burdensome and inflexible federal regulations which do not recognize particular needs and priorities of state and local governments. There is no matching requirement for benefit payments and the federal government pays most administrative costs.

While some of these programs have been in existence for a number of years (school lunch since 1946), expansions and new initiatives since 1966 have greatly broadened their scope and cost. Spending has grown from $1.2 billion in FY69 to an estimated $15.9 billion in FY81. Fraud, waste and abuse are a problem: benefit over-issuance in Food Stamps is estimated at $2.2 billion; benefits to non-needy children are estimated in the hundreds of millions of dollars under child nutrition and special milk programs.

Because the goal of these programs is to provide a basic human need -- food -- they are widely regarded as entitlements. Actually, except for child nutrition programs, funding for the USDA nutrition intervention programs is controllable through the appropriations process. Even the Food Stamp Program was capped in 1977. Nevertheless, Congress has yet to exercise its authority to limit program growth directly through the funding process for political reasons. In the meantime, since these programs are all indexed to price increases, further significant cost escalations can be expected.

Recommendation

That a comprehensive nutritional block grant program be proposed to replace the 13 individual categorical USDA programs. That the program be administered by the states under broad federal guidelines with limited planning and reporting requirements.

Regulation ☐ Approved ☒
Disapproved ☐
Legislation ☒ As Modified ☐

TRANSITION ACTION PAPER

WORK REQUIREMENT

Issue:

Should the Work Incentive (WIN) program be revamped to provide an effective work requirement? (WAGE)

Facts and Discussion:

The WIN program was enacted in 1967 in an attempt to deal with the growth in the AFDC rolls by providing new incentives for work, new work requirements for appropriate persons, and a work and training program to make the work incentives and work requirements meaningful. Even though the program has been amended several times, it has never accomplished its purpose. The work requirement has not been effective, and many employable individuals have been exempt from the program.

The WIN program has not been well-respected in the past, so it is recommended that the name be changed to remove the stigma of the program. WAGE (Work and Gainful Employment) is a suitable, positive acronym for a program which is designed to give people work experience and place them in regular employment whenever possible.

Registration in the WAGE program should be mandatory for all employable AFDC recipients; they should be required to seek and accept regular employment or to work in community work programs in the absence of regular jobs. If the individual refuses to comply, the welfare grant should be terminated for the entire family. Public and private employment agencies should be given financial incentives to place welfare recipients in regular employment.

Recommendation:

That the WIN program be revamped to require that employable AFDC recipients seek work, accept regular employment, and in the absence of such employment, participate in community work programs. That the program be renamed WAGE (Work and Gainful Employment).

Regulation ☒

Legislation ☒

Approved ☒
Disapproved ☐
As Modified ☐

TRANSITION ACTION PAPER

OVERLAPPING BENEFITS

OK
RR

Issue:

Should current law be amended to require the recognition of all cash of in-kind income available to the recipient of Aid to Families with Dependent Children, food stamps or other programs?

Facts and Discussion:

Numerous areas of overlap and duplication exist among the various public assistance porgrams now provided by the several levels of government. For example, food stamps provide a complete food supplement based upon a certain diet plan, yet duplicative assistance is provided through free noon meals to students, free school breakfasts in certain cases, summer feeding programs and other food programs. Similarly, Section 8 housing subsidies may be provided in addition to the deduction for shelter costs which is allowed in the determination of cash needs standards. The medical care component in cost-of-living indices may be retained while complete medical care is provided through the Medicaid program.

In other situations, individual living circumstances of recipients may provide the equivalent of in-kind income. For example, the needs of a pregnant woman with no other children may be less than two separate individuals yet, if aid is provided, it may now be calculated on the latter circumstance. Moreover, if two recipient families live together, there is no recognition now of economies of scale so full housing and utilities allowances (as if each were living separately) may be provided.

The extent of the savings realized may be most substantial, depending upon the extent of the overlap or recognition of other cash or in-kind income in any legislative changes. Proposed legislation, which would have eliminated a part of the duplication between food stamps and free or reduced price school lunches, was estimated to save $600 million in Federal funds annually.

Recommendation:

That legislation be submitted to require recognition of all cash or in-kind income available to recipients of various public assistance programs for purposes of determining benefits under those programs.

Regulation ☐

Legislation ☒

Approved ☒
Disapproved ☐
As Modified ☐

TRANSITION ACTION PAPER

DEDUCTION OF WORK RELATED EXPENSES

Issue

Should Aid to Families with Dependent Children (AFDC) regulations be amended to require that work-related expenses be deducted from income before, rather than after, the earned income disregard? (Net vs. gross)

Facts and Discussion

In late 1968, as part of the last minute changes of the outgoing Johnson Administration, Secretary Wilbur Cohen reversed the order in which earned income exemptions and work-related expenses are computed in the calculation of amounts which are not to be counted in the determination of income of a recipient in the AFDC program.

Under the order established in 1968, earned income exemptions are to be deducted first, and work-related expenses second; consequently one-third of work-related expenses are now deducted twice (because the first computation provides for exemption of one-third of remaining income after exemption of the first $30, and the second provides for deduction of 100% of work-related expenses).

Reversing the computation so that work-related expenses are deducted first would place the calculation in its proper order, and insure that one-third of the work-related expenses are not deducted twice.

Recommendation

That regulations be issued to require that the disregard be applied against gross rather than net income.

Regulation [x]

Legislation [x]

Approved [x]
Disapproved [ ]
As Modified [ ]

TRANSITION ACTION PAPER

EXCLUDED ASSETS

OK BC

Issue

Should changes be made in exemptions which are allowed under the current assets test for the Aid to Families with Dependent Children program?

Facts and Discussion

Under eligibility criteria currently applicable in the AFDC program, significant assets may be exempt from consideration in the determination of need. For example, an individual is allowed to have a house of any value and still be eligible for benefits. Personal property, including jewelry, furs, silver and other valuable items, is also wholly exempt. Automobiles (sometimes of limited value) and other items are also exempt from the assets test.

Absent compelling evidence to the contrary, possession of these items suggests that the applicant is not in sufficient need to turn to the taxpayers for support. At a minimum, taxpayers should not be expected to support individuals who are allowed to protect their assets for future use rather than convert them to cash to meet current needs.

Recommendation

That regulations be adopted to limit exempt assets.

Regulation [x]

Legislation [ ]

Approved [x]
Disapproved [ ]
As Modified [ ]

TRANSITION ACTION PAPER

MEDICAID MANDATES ON STATES

Issue

Should regulations be issued and legislation be submitted to eliminate mandates on states which add cost to the Medicaid program?

Facts and Discussion

Through regulation and statute, States are mandated to provide certain services in the Medicaid program. Some other mandates relate to cost control to eliminate errors and fraud. As long as Medicaid financing remains open-ended on a matching basis, the cost control mandates should be continued. The mandated services and coverage, however, should be repealed because states are in a better position than the federal government to make decisions related to services offered, coverage and their relative priorities. This is particularly true where state and federal budgets are tight as they are now.

Recommendation

The federal Medicaid regulations and statutory mandates, other than cost control mandates, be repealed.

Regulation ☒

Legislation ☒

Approved ☒

Disapproved ☐

As Modified ☐

TRANSITION ACTION PAPER

STREAMLINE HEARINGS PROCESSES

OK
PR

Issue

Should DHHS hearings processes be streamlined in anticipation of intentional "flooding" by opponents of welfare reform?

Facts and Discussion

With the exception of disability hearings (covered in a seperate action paper) there are roughly 50 types of hearings conducted by the Department of Health and Human Services.

Among these are various state plan hearings (AFDC, child support, Low Income Energy Assistance, Medicaid, Social Services, Aging and Developmental Disabilities);

Business/economic hearings (Medicaid and Medicare provider reimbursement, PSRO terminations and nonrenewals, suspension of practitioners, Public Health Services designations of service areas, HMO qualifications, FDA public hearings, regulatory hearings, environmental impact statement hearings, lab practices, and others).

Discrimination hearings (civil discrimination in receipt of public assistance, discrimination on the basis of age, handicap and sex).

Grants appeals (general grant programs, disallowance under state plans, PHS construction costs, Indian Health Services and Office of Human Development Services including Head Start, Native Americans and Indian Social Services and Nutritional Services).

There is considerable diffusion of responsibility, lack of accountability for management, performance and hearings policies. No single point in DHHS has oversight responsibility for hearings and appeals. Flexibility to deploy personnel to meet shifting workloads does not exist.

In the implementation of welfare reforms it can be expected that opponents will make every effort to "flood" the processes. The large number of processes currently in place are extremely vulnerable to massive appeals.

Recommendation

Yes. The office would have authority to implement periodic management reporting of all hearings processes, allocate hearings officers and staff to adjust to changing workloads, conduct quality control of decision quality; to improve and shorten hearings processes, and to insure the minimum hearings process providing due process.

Regulation	[X]	Approved	[X]
		Disapproved	[ ]
Legislation	[ ]	As Modified	[ ]

Bob Carleson is honored upon his retirement from the White House staff, April 16, 1984—from left to right: Jack Svahn, Ronald Reagan, Bob Carleson, and James M. Hall.

> Most welfare rights organizations have been more than willing to accept these . . . provisions in order to get the benefit floor they have never been able to achieve. Once the 65 percent minimum is law, they plan to begin working for periodic increases in the basic percentage rate, a drive with which [Congressman James] Corman is sympathetic. . . . It is this vision of a rising floor and a growing federal commitment that has generated most of the opposition to the bill.[11]

In fact, during the debate on the House floor on November 7, 1979, Congressman Conable declared his opposition to the Carter-Kennedy-Corman bill:

> I hope no one here thinks that the 65 percent figure will remain forever at that level. Just a few weeks ago I heard Arthur Burns remind us that a few prescient individuals opposed creating a federal income tax of 1 percent many years ago because they were sure that someday it would become confiscatory. They turned out to be right. I am afraid that I will be right when I say that the national minimum of 65 percent is just the beginning. . . . The bill leads the welfare program, in my opinion, in the wrong direction. It moves us several steps closer to the uniform, national income redistribution program sought by many who have been active in the welfare area for a decade or longer.[12]

---

11. Alan Ehrenhalt, "Minimum Welfare Payment Nears House Showdown," the *Washington Star,* October 28, 1979.
12. *Congressional Record*, November 7, 1979, H10285–6.

The Carter-Kennedy-Corman bill then moved to the Senate Finance Committee, where it met strong opposition in the form of the Long-Dole Bill (S. 1382), the companion bill to the Conable-Rousselot Bill (H.R. 4460). The situation in the Senate, however, was much different from that in the House. S. 1382 had the strong bipartisan sponsorship of Chairman Long and ranking Republican Bob Dole of the Finance Committee, as well as other key senators: Bob Packwood (R-OR), Herman Talmadge (D-GA), Richard Schweiker (R-PA), S. I. Hayakawa (R-CA), and David Boren (D-OK). Senator Schweiker was the ranking Republican on the Labor and Human Resources Committee.

To have an *efficient* and *effective* system of income redistribution, it was necessary to eliminate complexity and introduce uniformity. But to have a *decent* welfare system, it was necessary to meet the basic needs of those who, through no fault of their own, needed public assistance. Welfare policy is complicated and complex by its nature, which is why it cannot effectively be developed or administered at the federal level. This is why the two choices of welfare reform would lead us in opposite directions. One direction was toward federalization, federal policy decisions, federal benefit levels, and an efficient system of federal income redistribution. The other direction was toward a need-based welfare program that would move decisions from Washington to the state capitols, city halls, and county courthouses.

In 1980, these were the stark alternatives before Congress and the nation.

6

End Running

During Ronald Reagan's 1980 presidential primary campaign, and later during the Reagan/Bush campaign, I served as an unpaid senior policy advisor. In addition, I chaired the Reagan/Bush welfare reform task force. The task force never met, but two close associates, my consulting firm partner Carl Williams and John Findley of the Pacific Legal Foundation, assisted me in preparing the task force report. It was, in effect, a compilation of over thirty proposed changes in the federal welfare code which I had been gathering since late 1970. Most of the changes involved closing loopholes that the incremental redistributionists had opened over the years in the guise of "work incentives." Getting rid of these loopholes would remove non-needy persons from the welfare rolls.

During the 1980–81 presidential transition, I first served as director of the transition team at the Department of Health and Human Services (HHS, formerly HEW), and later at the transition headquarters in the policy development office. Among my responsibilities at HHS was that of receiving the three campaign task force reports: social security, headed by Rita Ricardo-Campbell; health, headed by William Walsh; and welfare reform, headed by me. The social security and health reports had been leaked to the press and were public knowledge. I had held the welfare reform report very closely and refused repeated efforts by the press to leak it. I found that my next responsibility was to forward the welfare reform task force report to policy headquarters, so I offered my services there and passed it on to myself.

I converted the recommendations in the report into a decision-book for a major Reagan welfare reform. Using Reagan's California decision format of one issue per page—with check boxes for "approved," "disapproved," and "approved as amended"—the loose-leaf book contained over thirty-five items. All but three of the items were to be included in the initial welfare reform effort. The three to be used in a second effort in the following congressional term were to turn the AFDC, Food Stamp, and Medicaid programs into finite block grants to the states with a minimum of federal rules.

At my request, transition chief Ed Meese arranged a welfare reform "decision meeting" at Blair House in Washington on January 6, 1981. In attendance were the president-elect, secretary of HHS–designate Richard Schweiker, my associate Carl Williams, and about ten or twelve others. (Meese himself could not attend.) Some of the attendees would come and go from time to time.

I made the presentation to the president-elect. In my opinion, only Ronald Reagan, Carl Williams, and I really knew what was being presented *en toto*. The three of us had become intimately acquainted with the details of true welfare reform in California in 1971 and 1972. Reagan understood clearly each item, and he was enthusiastic. He checked the "approved" box on each policy item and initialed each page. Two items were amended. At Reagan's request, workfare for AFDC was to be enlarged to include workfare for food stamps. At the request of Secretary-designate Schweiker, a proposed assistant secretary for welfare in the Department of Health and Human Services was deferred. All other items were approved as I submitted them. "It's really fun to be making decisions again," the president-elect declared as the meeting progressed. The items to block grant the AFDC, Food Stamp, and Medicaid programs were approved by Reagan, but were held for the following session of the Congress.

In April or May 1981, Reagan approved our recommendation to move the program as a major initiative. I asked John Findley to draft the legislation.

After the inauguration and the internal White House budgeting process, it became clear to me that Office of Management and Budget Director David Stockman's legislative strategy would be "the only game in town" for early public policy efforts. Stockman planned to use budget reconciliation for substantive legislation and to use the House conservative Democrats and Republicans to "roll" the House Democratic leadership.

When, as special assistant to the president for policy development, I heard the rumor that the president's approved draft budget fell short by about $3 billion due to a totaling error, I took the welfare reform proposals to Dave Stockman. I informed him that they had been approved by the president-elect in January, that they totaled at least $3 billion in savings, that the legislation had been drafted, and that he could plug the reforms into the budget "like a cassette."

Stockman accepted the offer, and the budget was printed and ready for public announcement when a *Washington Post* front-page Sunday story headlined that "workfare" was to be proposed by the president in his forthcoming budget. I watched the news that evening to see what the president's reaction would be when asked the workfare question as he arrived from Camp David by helicopter. "Mr. President," a reporter asked, "is it true that you will be proposing workfare in your budget?" His answer: "I'm for workfare."

Monday morning I went to my White House office fully prepared for the onslaught from the David Gergens, Richard Darmans, and other erstwhile Reagan opponents who had never supported his type of welfare reform, but who were now on his staff as James Baker's people. Assistant to the President Martin Anderson called me to say that they were blaming me for "end running" the president and would I please come over to defend myself. I did. At our meeting, they claimed that I did not have the president's approval. I responded that indeed I did have his approval, and produced photocopies of the pertinent pages from the president-elect's decision-book containing his approval checks and initials. Reagan had given his original decision-book back to me at the conclusion of the meeting, with instructions to implement his decisions at the appropriate time. I produced also the detailed written record of the Blair House decision meeting. At the time of the decision meeting, Reagan's White House staff had yet to be selected. I had expected this kind of opposition, and saw to it that a detailed record be kept and copies sent to those who had attended the Blair House meeting. Gergen, Darman, et al declared that these decisions did not count because Reagan was not president when he made them. I said they did count, and I challenged them to come with me into the Oval Office and make their arguments directly to the president. They demurred, saying it was too late anyway, that the budget had been printed. That is how President Reagan's major welfare reform reached Congress in its pure state.

The budget sailed through the Senate with the reform features intact, supported by Finance Committee Chairman Bob Dole and Senator Russell Long, with whom I had been working for years. I told Dave Stockman to leave the Senate welfare language intact so that if he succeeded in rolling over the House leadership the welfare reform language would be identical in both bills and therefore not subject to change by the conference committee, which would be hostile on the House side. The Gramm-Latta Budget Reconciliation Bill was passed over the opposition of the House leadership. The Senate members of the conference committee insisted on following the rule that identical language was not subject to the conference. Thus the historic Reagan welfare program decided upon at Blair House became law, hidden away in the massive Budget Reconciliation Act of 1981, unnoticed by the press or by our dogged opposition.

After the dust settled, our opponents predicted in the media that the hundreds of thousands of welfare recipients in families where the principal member was working would stay on or return to the rolls because the worker would quit working rather than be removed from welfare as it was provided in the reforms. Many of our conservative economists made the same prediction because of the "prohibitive marginal tax rate" imposed by the reforms. I had been arguing for years that the same high marginal "tax rate" disincentives that would reduce work effort at the high-income end of the earning spectrum would not exist at the low-income end because the incentives to break out of poverty would prevail. Two years after the 1981 welfare reforms took effect, several exhaustive research studies found that there had been no significant reduction in work effort on the part of those made ineligible by our reforms. On the contrary, the number of hours worked increased and income increased as these families were freed from the welfare system.

The most significant of these studies was the Research Triangle Institute's "Final Report: Evaluation of the 1981 AFDC Amendments," dated April 15, 1983, and submitted to the Department of Health and Human Services.

For years the redistributionists had been selling conservatives on "strengthening work incentives" as the argument for moving welfare eligibility into the range where income was low but sufficient to meet basic family needs. They argued that these "work incentives" would encourage nonworking welfare families to work. In practice, no significant number of nonworking families went to work, but millions more persons were made eligible for AFDC. This resulted in the tremendous growth of welfare rolls in the late 1960s and early 1970s. In later years, I heard conservative Republicans and others falling for these arguments once again. They bought into the notion that it was possible to "remove work disincentives" by letting people earn more and "save more" and retain their eligibility for a cash welfare grant. In 1993, the same siren call of the early 1960s which led to the excesses of the late '60s and '70s was being heard again. As George Santayana famously remarked, "Those who cannot remember the past are condemned to repeat it."

The proposals approved by President Reagan at Blair House for later block grants in AFDC, food stamps, and Medicaid were scuttled by the Jim Baker side of the White House, although we were able to enact block grants for social services and some other services in 1982. Through the second Reagan term Congress nibbled away at the 1981 reforms. A massive, dubious Moynihan-inspired social services program improperly disguised as work-related was passed and signed. The nibbling continued under President George H. W. Bush, but the 1981 AFDC reforms remained substantially in effect.

Shifting Opinion?

It was pleasing to note the shift occurring among opinion leaders during the 1980s. Jonathan Yardley of the *Washington Post* reviewed Lawrence Mead's 1986 book

Beyond Entitlement, and it now seemed *fashionable* to believe that welfare—"free money," so to speak—carried undesirable consequences. It was time for some mechanism to be developed by which recipients could earn the benefits provided.

Another article in the *Washington Post*, by William Raspberry, related his remedy of the problem through the discovery of an obscure writing by Alexis de Tocqueville on the fact that public welfare, which he called "public charity," perpetuates idleness on the majority of the poor and provides for their leisure at the expense of those who worked.

Finally, a quote from a 1978 conference impressed me years later. It concerned the perversity of our welfare system:

> We go to a young girl, who's now 18 or 16 or even younger and this is what we say, "abandon all of your hopes, your schools will not teach you, you will not learn to read or write, you will never have a decent job, you will live in the neighborhoods of endless unemployment and poverty with drugs and violence," but then we say to this child, "wait, there is a way, one way, you can be somebody to someone, that will give you an apartment and furniture to fill it; we will give you a TV set and telephone, we will give you clothing and cheap food and free medical care and some spending money besides, and in turn you only have to do one thing, that is go out there and have a baby."

The man who said that was Senator Edward Kennedy, in an address before the annual conference of the

Michigan NAACP in Detroit. When this was first read to me, my guesses were that the author was almost anyone other than Edward Kennedy, particularly in 1978.

The years of discussion of welfare brought about general agreement on some matters. One was that welfare can cause dependency. Secondly, dependency is bad and it hurts people. We also moved toward consensus on the point that people who are able should be expected to *earn* their benefits.

7

Working Principles

By the end of Ronald Reagan's terms in Sacramento and Washington, we were eager to see welfare reform implemented across the nation. True welfare reform would be based on eight guiding principles.

Principle # 1
No honest work is demeaning.

Some social planners and activists tell us that certain jobs are "demeaning" or "dead-end." Such talk is elitist. It is a disservice to the millions of Americans who fill those jobs. Many millions of other Americans have done these jobs in the past, gaining work experience, and as a result have progressed to more advanced work. Millions of aliens, legal or illegal, are now filling many of these jobs, and as a result will advance into more responsible and higher-paying jobs. Meanwhile, millions of nonimmigrant Americans are discouraged from taking these jobs because they are called demeaning or dead-end.

Older Americans remember the time when a person felt that his or her services were worth paying money for, whether mowing lawns, delivering newspapers, washing dishes, caring for children, cleaning house, or harvesting crops. Now, the elitists consider this work demeaning.

I am told by those who know that a hardworking, dependable restaurant dishwasher is in demand for promotion to busman, waiter, and captain. And in America, one never knows whether today's dishwasher will start his or her own restaurant tomorrow. If a "dead-end" job is defined as one where promotion is not possible, what about the police patrolmen, schoolteachers, factory workers, clerks, salespersons, and others who spend their entire careers in the same position? These workers know the satisfaction of a job well done, and they are supporting themselves and their families while contributing usefully to their community.

In a productive society, only a relatively few people can become leadmen, foremen, supervisors, or executives. The important thing is not that everyone makes it to a more responsible position. The important thing is that everyone has the opportunity to do so.

Today, many young people lack the incentive to accept an entry level job which entails hard work in less-than-comfortable circumstances. Who of us would? If we provide income to our young people *without* work, it is only natural that many will choose not to work. And it's then that they miss the opportunity for future success. If a young man or woman is discouraged from taking a job that would provide valuable work experience and promote good work habits—habits that are necessary in our competitive marketplace—the victim is that young person, and society. All because the opportunity for future success was said to be demeaning.

Principle #2

For an able-bodied person to take something for nothing is demeaning.

In a free society based on the Judeo-Christian work ethic, each of us has the right to live our own lives in freedom as long as we don't impinge on the rights of others. We may or may not have children, as we choose. We may travel as we choose. We are obligated, however, to support ourselves and our children to the best of our ability. That is the price of our freedom.

We also have an obligation to provide for common needs through our taxes. It is right that we support those in our society who, through adversity or misfortune, *cannot* help themselves. No responsible American would have it any other way. So productive citizens pay taxes to support the disabled.

However, if an able-bodied person does not do everything he can to support himself and his family, and instead takes support from others who are, he debases and demeans himself. He demeans himself in the eyes of his family, of his community, and of himself.

Encouraging dependence moves us towards totalitarianism—when government decides that a respectable working person who is supporting his family with pride is not providing *enough*—and that he is therefore guaranteed a "sufficient" income from government. He loses his self-respect and the respect of his family.

Principle #3

Neither the economy nor the poor can survive in a system which pays able-bodied people to do nothing.

We hear much about how the millions of illegal aliens working in the country are being exploited and that the vast majority take jobs that "Americans don't want." These often are jobs in restaurants, hotels, and agriculture that pay at, or just above, the minimum wage. At the same time, employers are always complaining that they cannot find willing, reliable workers, even in our central cities, where unemployment rates are high.

I believe that this is largely due to the fact that we structured a welfare system that paid able-bodied people for doing nothing—often more than they could take home at many entry-level jobs. And many employers, especially small business owners, could not compete with these high welfare benefits. As a result, private-sector jobs were lost or just not created.

A federal guaranteed-income program, as proposed in the past by the Nixon and Carter administrations, would have been a massive move in the same direction. It would increase the pressures on future congresses to continually increase minimum benefits. The process would continue until the nation's economy collapsed. Instead of the poor getting more, *everyone* would get less.

Principle #4
Welfare work incentives don't work.

"We should make work pay more than welfare."

"We should provide work incentives to encourage welfare recipients to go to work."

"Why should a welfare recipient go to work if she gets a dollar-for-dollar reduction in her welfare grant if she does?"

These are statements we heard repeatedly from the 1960s through the early 1990s. But the "solutions" of the '60s resulted in disastrous unintended consequences.

I suppose that if I had been in Congress in the 1960s, I too would have voted to make work attractive to welfare recipients by not counting work-related expenses as income. Such deductions were called "earned income disregards" in welfare terminology. It was common sense, but in this case the "common sense" was wrong.

When Governor Reagan asked me to examine California's welfare policy, I was appalled at the way "work-related expenses" had been defined in state regulations. The definition had been broadened to include just about anything that could conceivably be claimed as work-related. The child-care expense income disregards had been similarly broadened. When I led the California

Department of Social Welfare in 1971, we tightened the state regulation on work-related and child care expense income disregards, and as a result, we removed many families from the AFDC rolls. I noticed that taking this action did not cause these families to quit work because of the loss of the "work incentive." Most of the working families that remained on the rolls were there because of the federally required $30 and one-third monthly income disregard (the amount of income that is not counted as "income" for welfare eligibility purposes).

Then, in 1974, the Michigan Department of Social Services published a report showing that the federal income disregard had not caused a significant number of AFDC recipients to go to work. In fact, it had caused a major increase in the rolls and costs. Because of the 1967 income disregards policy, a great number of working families were made eligible for AFDC at higher income levels.[1]

We finally did something about the federal income disregards when Ronald Reagan became president. I wrote the 1981 Reagan AFDC reforms to reverse the unintended consequences of the 1967 reforms.[2] First, we removed the federal prohibition on states requiring AFDC recipients to earn or "work off" the grant. Among other changes, we tightened the work-related expense and child-care income disregards. We restricted the $30 and one-third disregard to the first four

1. See Vernon K. Smith, *Welfare Work Incentives—The Earnings Exemption and Its Impact on AFDC Employment, Earnings, and Program Cost*, Michigan Department of Social Services, 1974.
2. The Work Incentive (WIN) program (P.L. 90-248).

months of employment as a "start-up" supplement for items such as new clothes or a move to a new apartment closer to work.

Following the passage of the 1981 Reagan AFDC reforms, even friendly conservative economists predicted that the approximately 300,000 families removed from the rolls by the elimination of the permanent income disregards would quit work because of the new "high marginal tax rates." As I had expected, the families did not quit work. Free of welfare dependency, they worked more, and their earned incomes increased. This was the finding of the aforementioned Research Triangle of North Carolina study commissioned by the federal government and issued April 15, 1983, two years after the reforms became law.[3]

The Research Triangle study was the subject of an article by Nicholas Lemann in the September 1984 issue of the *Atlantic Monthly.* Lemann noted that I was the single welfare expert of note who had predicted that the former recipients would keep working. Revisionists claimed that the Triangle study should have been conducted a year later, since before the 1981 reforms 17 percent of welfare recipients were working; three years later, only 3 percent were working.[4] Well, as they say in the country, "That dog won't hunt." Working families that had been on the welfare rolls exhibited that they really did not need welfare. Others like them were no longer permitted to come on the rolls.

---

3. See Research Triangle Institute, *Final Report Evaluation of the 1981 AFDC Amendments*, April 15, 1983.
4. Robert Moffitt, "Incentive, Effects of the U.S. Welfare System: A Review," *Journal of Economic Literature* (1992).

Despite the success of the 1981 Reagan reforms, we almost committed the mistakes of 1967 all over again. Several of the state demonstration projects—some with Republican governors—reintroduced continuing the earned income disregards. They told the tired old story about incentives for AFDC recipients to go to work. After all, it was plain common sense.

Federally imposed work requirements simply don't work. A discerning observer of bureaucracy could have figured that out even before the first welfare check for income disregards was cut. The implementing regulations were issued by federal bureaucrats who were institutionally opposed to requiring work. The regulations were full of definitions, exceptions, conditions, excessive child care standards, and other provisions guaranteed to make the congressionally imposed "work requirement" unworkable.

But apparently Republicans in Congress were ignorant of the lessons of "work incentives." The original 1993 House Republican welfare bill, H.R. 3500, as well as the 1994 Clinton welfare reform bill, reintroduced even larger continuing disregards than the federally mandated $30 and one-third. This time they were advocating a $200 plus a one-half deduction from gross monthly income before determining eligibility and grant level for AFDC. I suppose that the supporters of the increased disregards thought that the failure of the $30 and one-third was that it was not attractive enough—so let's try $200 plus half.

The fact is, it would never be enough. We learned from the massive federally run Seattle-Denver and New Jersey income maintenance experiments of the early

1970s that increasing the size of the earned income disregard to 50 percent had no appreciable effect on work effort. We knew from the post-1967 experience that a mere one-third income disregard resulted in a tremendous increase in welfare rolls and costs. The projected costs of the new disregard proposals were grossly underestimated. They would cost many *billions* of dollars per year more than the proponents claimed. Advocates for the disregards said that they would simply be an option for the states, that they would be available only to those already on the rolls, and that they would cause only a small increase in costs.

Well, we knew one thing from twenty-four years of experience with such promises: These were paper barriers. It's not easy to stop the momentum of government once it starts "helping" people. After a while, government welfare programs that are supposedly for our good can end up hurting us. And with income disregards in the guise of "work incentives," welfare rolls and costs expand rapidly, bringing millions more people into welfare dependency, and adding many billions of dollars in costs.

Principle #5

Those who are not physically able to support themselves should receive adequate living benefits.

The states should determine the definition of work and who should be required to perform it. The states' voters will enforce it.

The American people do not expect their welfare system to provide benefits to those who won't help themselves. My experience has shown me that many able-bodied welfare recipients will find jobs when it is made clear to them that they are expected to earn their benefits.

So we owe it to those who are not physically or mentally able to support themselves to provide adequate benefits. People of advanced age or with permanent and total disability, who are unable to support themselves, should receive welfare, particularly during inflationary times when their fixed incomes, if any, cannot keep pace with higher costs of the necessities of life. I believe that the Supplementary Security Income program for the aged, which Congress enacted in 1972, has moved us very close to solving this problem. (However, the similar program for the disabled is full of abuse and should be returned to the states.)

Principle #6

> ***Those who are not physically able to support themselves should be required and assisted to take treatment or training which may lead to partial or complete self-sufficiency.***

Many who are disabled can be retrained or rehabilitated to become productive members of society. Others, through treatment or training, or with supportive services, can become self-sufficient, free of need for institutionalization. Successes in this area reinforce the dignity of the individual, boosting individual self-respect and avoiding the high costs to the public of institutional care.

Principle #7

Those who have children should support their children—mother or father, married or not.

In our society, the freedom to conceive or bear children carries with it the responsibility to provide support. Many mothers with children at home are working to support themselves and their children or to contribute to their family income. I believe that a mother on welfare has as great an obligation to support her children as does the father. The success of our child support program for absent parents has strengthened this principle as it relates to the absent parent. We must do more to see that able-bodied single parents support themselves and their children. Many mothers with several children can provide child care for one or two more in order to free other mothers for work. Once working, a mother can move toward total self-support and, we hope, break the welfare cycle for her family.

Principle #8

Only the states, working through local and private entities, can solve the welfare problem.

I am convinced that a welfare system that embraces the guiding principles I have just stated cannot be designed or run from Washington—particularly not from the Department of Health and Human Services. Determining whether someone is able-bodied or not, working or not, absent or not, or how best to provide work, child care, or supportive services, requires effort and knowledge found only in the state or community where the people live. Benefits or work availability should start when need starts, and benefits should end when need ends. Benefit levels should meet basic needs only, and should not compete with an area's prevailing wages for those who are able-bodied.

Justice Brandeis once referred to the states as "laboratories of democracy." But the old funding structure of the AFDC program minimized the incentive for states to make their programs more effective. The federal government assumed a large portion (50 to 80 percent) of state costs on a completely open-ended basis. The savings which a state realized by eliminating an ineligible individual or by placing an eligible individual in a job were considerably reduced by this funding design. Proposals to provide fiscal relief to states by increasing matching formulas would only have worsened this situation.

By using a block-grant approach, however, the incentive could be reversed. The amount of the grant could be established at the level necessary to replace the open-ended federal funding amount. That grant level, once established for a state, would be a fixed amount each year guaranteed to the state, without regard to increases or decreases in the state's caseload. This would give each state the strongest possible incentive to improve the operation and structure of its program. If an ineligible person were kept off the rolls, or an eligible person given a job, the full amount saved would be available to the state to use for increasing the grants to eligible persons, or for whatever purpose the state found appropriate for its needy population.

The United States is unique with its fifty individual political entities. Each state has executive, legislative, and judicial branches; each state has the ability, independently, to raise revenues; each has the authority to make laws—all subject to an electorate. Of course, all of the states are also subject to the U.S. Constitution, the Bill of Rights, the Civil Rights Act and the Voting Rights Act, among other federal constraints. These later acts and the reapportionment decision of the Supreme Court successfully transformed the southern states so that today everyone has the vote and it counts.

The same people who elect presidents, senators, and representatives elect governors and state legislators. They can be trusted to protect their truly needy residents. Indeed, *only* they can be trusted.

8

Naysayers

After Ronald Reagan became president, his councillor and former California chief of staff, Ed Meese, attempted to duplicate the California cabinet decision system by creating cabinet councils, consisting of cabinet members in several different subject-matter areas of public policy. This did not succeed as planned, because implementation was left largely to people who actively had opposed Ronald Reagan and his policies. Decisions would be made in a cabinet council by the president and later "unmade" by people who were long-time opponents of Reagan's views, under the direction of James Baker and Richard Darman. Baker had been the campaign manager of the only anti-Reagan primary candidate, George H. W. Bush, a campaign that blamed Reagan for Gerald Ford's defeat in 1976. Darman had been a long-time sidekick of former HEW secretary Elliot Richardson and was one of Richardson's key aides in opposition to Reagan's California welfare reform. He later served in Jimmy Carter's administration as ambassador to the law of the sea conference, Elliott Richardson's deputy. He never was a Reagan man. He, Baker, and David Gergen would argue that they were simply pragmatists, because even Republicans in Congress would not support the Reagan policies.

Ronald Reagan had proved in California, however, that he could go to the people and overcome opposition in the legislature from Democrats and Republicans alike. Not only was this the case with welfare reform, but also with his tax rebates of 1974. The major gains as president in 1981 were the Budget Reconciliation Act, with its welfare reform, and the tax cuts enacted before Jim Baker and Dick Darman could get control. These important policies were achieved in spite of a hostile House leadership. So it could be done if everyone in the administration was loyal to the president.

As the executive secretary of the cabinet council on human resources, I encouraged a healthy airing of views to allow the president the opportunity to make the most informed decision possible.

However, some of the White House cabinet councils allowed a member to lobby other members to support his or her position on an issue in order to present a united front to the president. This practice deprived Reagan of opposing views or other options and could lead to decisions that he did not prefer.

An example was a joint cabinet council meeting in late 1982 when Secretary of Transportation Drew Lewis made a proposal for a five-cent increase in the gas tax, with one cent earmarked for mass transit. No one spoke in opposition. Normally I would not have entered the meeting until it had reached the agenda of the cabinet council on human resources, but I had been permitted to arrive early because I was recovering from major heart surgery and could not manage to get from my office to the Cabinet Room on short notice.

The joint meeting was chaired by the president. Secretary Lewis knew of President Reagan's general opposition to tax increases. I found out later from Secretary Lewis's deputy Darrell Trent that Lewis had lobbied the other members to support or at least to not object to his proposal.

I had not been concentrating on the meeting because I was conserving energy for my issue. But slowly I realized that the topic was a familiar one from California days when I had been Reagan's highway department appointee and we, together, had fought the use of highway-user taxes for mass transit. Reagan had been frowning throughout Lewis's presentation because it called for a higher gas tax, but no one made an issue of the proposed diversion to mass transit.

Perhaps I shouldn't have, but I raised my finger to the president's attention. I was sitting across the table from him against the wall. He noticed and asked me for my views on the subject. I told him that I was not in a position to remark on the need for an increase on the gas tax, but I reminded him of our opposition over twelve years before to highway users' taxes being diverted to mass transit, and suggested that he continue to oppose it. He smiled, remarked to all in the room about our California experience, and then and there said no to one cent or any cents to mass transit, even if it was necessary to get an increase in the gas tax.

When the meeting was over, Elizabeth Dole, who was then assistant to the president for public liaison, whispered to me with a smile that I was "losing the sympathy vote," and I never knew whether or not she favored the gas-tax diversion. This is both an example of the wisdom of presenting all views to Reagan and an example of how the Baker camp did not work successfully on the president's behalf. When the legislation finally came down from Congress, the diversion to mass transit was there and they had committed the president to sign it.

Ronald Reagan was a success as president, in spite of Baker, Darman, et al. They showed their true colors when, in early 1989, after running a winning George H. W. Bush campaign based on Reagan values, they cleaned house of loyal Reagan appointees much more efficiently than had Carter when he succeeded Ford, and would Clinton when he succeeded Bush. (My wife, Susan, was one of the "cleansed.") They then proceeded to reverse many of the Reagan policies, including breaking Bush's promise of "read my lips, no new taxes," a reversal that was engineered by Dick Darman.

Moynihan's "Reform"

After the successful 1981 Reagan welfare reforms tightened welfare eligibility, Senator Daniel Patrick Moynihan pushed a new "reform" through Congress in 1988.

The reform, known as the JOBS program,[1] had been advertised as requiring work. Instead, it gave the federal government more control over welfare in the states and created new social service bureaucracies.

Moynihan promised that the 1988 reform would steer welfare mothers into work and off the rolls. It was praised by Democrats and some Republicans alike as a final means of reducing welfare dependency. The Reagan White House had been promising a veto until George H. W. Bush, the Republican presidential candidate, pulled the rug out from under them by supporting Moynihan's version of the bill just as the House and Senate conferees were to meet to work out the final version. Reagan signed the bill on October 13, 1988, less than a month before the presidential election. The driving force behind the legislation was the chairman of the National Governors Association, Bill Clinton, along with Moynihan. But Bush's support made it bipartisan.

By 1988 I was no longer on the White House staff, having left in 1984 to return to private life, but in an article published in the conservative weekly *Human Events,* I predicted that the proposed legislation would cause an explosive growth in the welfare rolls instead of the reductions in the rolls promised by its authors. The lone senator to vote against the final passage of the legislation, Jesse Helms of North Carolina, made the same prediction on the Senate floor.

I had based my predictions on the Moynihan bill provisions that would loosen some of the tough eligibility requirements enacted in the 1981 Reagan welfare re-

---

1. The Job Opportunities and Basic Skills (JOBS) training program was part of the Family Support Act of 1988 (P.L. 100-485).

forms. For instance, mandating the two-parent family program; providing waivers which would make it possible to reverse more of the 1981 reforms; permitting waivers to redefine "unemployed" by basing it on income earned instead of hours worked per month; promising strict "work requirements," which really would not work in practice, but which could be avoided by having another child under the age of six; and promising education, training, and other attractive social services such as child care and medical services after leaving the welfare rolls, the sole price of admission being to have a first child. Even though the incentives engendered by each of these elements may have been slight, taken together they would cause dramatic growth in the AFDC rolls.

Our predictions came true. The nation's AFDC rolls exploded. Defenders of the 1988 reforms pointed to the recession as the cause. But this was not the case. Consider the AFDC rolls during the 1982 recession. After President Reagan's 1981 welfare reforms reduced the AFDC rolls by over 800,000 people, the recession of 1982 was contained and the AFDC rolls did not reach the pre-Reagan level until after the enactment of the 1988 Moynihan welfare reform.

Moynihan—sociologist, former UN ambassador, and veteran of LBJ's War on Poverty—was the Senate's "leading expert" on welfare. Several times during the welfare reform debate of the mid-1990s, Moynihan admitted that the JOBS program "has not worked as well as we expected, but we should build on it."

"Has not worked as well as we expected" was the understatement of the year, maybe the decade. After the

JOBS program was implemented in 1990, the AFDC rolls did not go down as promised. Instead, they grew by an additional 3,233,000 people by 1994; that's 3.2 million more Americans who became trapped in welfare dependency.

But Senator Moynihan found other excuses for the AFDC increase. He relied on studies conducted by bureaucratic entities which were a part of the problem in the first place. At a Senate Finance Committee hearing on a Congressional Budget Office study, Senator Moynihan cited the study as proof that the increase in the AFDC rolls was caused by the 1990 recession and increased illegitimacy, particularly involving young single mothers. In any event, the only significant happening in 1988–89 relating to AFDC was Moynihan and Governor Clinton's "welfare reform."

This fact would prove relevant in 1995. The Daschle-Moynihan "welfare reform" bill went before the Senate with backing by President Clinton and the Children's Defense Fund. It was disguised as a tough five-years-and-out bill. It was not. It built on the failed reforms of 1988. The Republicans had been fooled by Clinton and Moynihan in 1988. They would not be fooled again.

Bush-Clinton

About three months into the Bush administration in 1989, my wife, Susan, and I paid a courtesy call on Ronald Reagan in his Century City office. After showing us around his office, he asked how things were going in Washington. I told him that it was not good, that the Bush administration had gotten rid of all the Reaganites in the administration and were now working on changing his policies.

He responded, "I can't believe that George would do that."

I said that I was not saying that George Bush himself even knew of what was going on, but that his administration was made up primarily of people from the Ford administration who held Reagan responsible for Ford's loss to Carter, especially Jim Baker and Dick Darman.

He repeated that he could not believe that George would do this. On our way out I told Kathy Osborne, his assistant, that he did not believe me about what the Bush administration was doing to his people and policies. A few months later she called to tell me that "he believes you now."

Bill Clinton simply continued down the road George Bush had followed. He even gave David Gergen the same position in the White House he had occupied in the Jim Baker wing of the Reagan White House. It was not twelve years of Reagan/Bush, as Bill Clinton claimed. It was eight years of Reagan followed by twelve years of Bush/Clinton. Moreover, much of the domestic policy had George Bush's fingerprints on it, especially the disastrous Governor Clinton-Senator Moynihan–inspired welfare reform of 1988. Only the 1996 welfare reform bill—passed three times by a Reaganite Congress, vetoed twice, and signed reluctantly by Bill Clinton as reelection insurance—was a true Reagan initiative.

In the meantime, incremental efforts to attain the three conditions of efficient redistribution had made more and more groups eligible for AFDC. One group that gained eligibility was intact working families. How? By defining "unemployed" by the amount of monthly income earned rather than by the number of hours worked. In Bill Clinton's early administration, a state could get a quick statewide waiver to replace the one-hundred-hour rule definition of "unemployed" with an income rule. At the same time, that state faced a wait of two years or forever to get a waiver for a family cap or limit, and then it would only get it for only one or two counties. Waivers to expand welfare were given quickly, while statewide waivers to restrict welfare were granted after much delay, and then only on a limited basis with impossible conditions.

Other incremental changes included a national minimum-benefit level in AFDC and a cash-out of the Food Stamp Program. The Food Stamp Program already had two of the three legs of the stool in place: universal eligibility and benefits levels set by Congress. If the benefits were to be given in cash instead of food stamps, the last leg would be in place, and off we would go to efficient income redistribution.

How to End Welfare as We Knew It

In the mid-1990s, the states administered three open-ended personal entitlement welfare programs financed in whole or in part with federal funds and subject to federal controls and requirements. These programs were (and are) Aid to Families with Dependent Children (AFDC), the Food Stamp Program, and Medicaid. Until 1972, the welfare program for the totally and permanently disabled, (later known as SSID) was administered by the states in a manner similar to AFDC. But since the SSID program moved to federal administration it was severely abused and was used by many of the states as a dumping ground for more than a few of their welfare cases. It was past time that this program be returned to the states.

These four programs needed to be replaced by clean block grants to the states. The debates in Congress over these programs took the form of either keeping the personal entitlement with federal controls while "fixing" and expanding them, the traditional Democratic Party solution; or turning all or some of them over to the states as block grants, the House Republican solution. The block grant solution, however, evolved into a debate between the Hamiltonian conservatives and the Jeffersonian conservatives.

Ronald Reagan was a Jeffersonian conservative. He knew that the federal government should not be dictating to the states. He long supported clean block grants to the states from the treasury department, bypassing the federal welfare bureaucracies.

The clean block grant proposals had these features:

- The AFDC, Food Stamp, Medicaid, and SSID programs were each to be replaced with a clean block grant in a finite appropriation based on the amount of federal funds received for the program in the most recent year.
- Each block grant was to go to the states directly from the treasury department, thereby bypassing

the departments of Health and Human Services and Agriculture, making their related bureaucracies unnecessary. The food-stamp block could be made in the form of food coupons, to ensure that they were spent only on food.

- Each block grant was to assure federal justice department protection of basic civil rights.
- Each block grant was to require periodic reports to the public and audits by independent auditors approved by the governor and the secretary of the treasury, to ensure that the funds were spent only for the purposes of the grant.
- The AFDC block grant was to specify the general purposes of the grant, including reducing illegitimacy, requiring work, and keeping families intact. However, these were to be simply goals, not requirements. All definitions and interpretations could be made by state law.
- The Medicaid program was to be designated to provide health services to needy persons in the state. The states were to make all decisions regarding need, methods, and types of services.
- The same simple purposes could be made for the Food Stamp and SSID programs.

These clean block grants met the Jeffersonian standards of maximum state discretion, while limiting the federal funds available each fiscal year. Each state could end welfare as they knew it. The states could replace the broken system with a new system that reflected the values, needs and desires of their people. Cleared of the federal shield, the state bureaucrats would be faced with a stark choice: either perform as the voters intended or be replaced through the ballot box.

9

THE CLASS OF '94 DEBATE

Until President Lyndon Johnson sought to establish his Great Society, welfare in America was primarily a state, local, and private responsibility. Federal welfare spending was modest. But following Washington's takeover of welfare during the 1960s' War on Poverty, government welfare spending soared. By the mid-1990s, government at all levels spent over $350 billion per year on welfare, more than on national defense. Between 1965 and 1995, government had spent $5.4 trillion on welfare for the poor. Yet the 1995 poverty rate of 15.1 percent was higher than the 14.7 percent in 1966 when the War on Poverty began.

In the early '90s things were beginning to change, with new Reagan-style governors like Tommy Thompson of Wisconsin determined to reduce their welfare rolls and use the work requirements permitted in the Reagan reform of 1981.

But the real revolution came with the election of 1994. All the big states, except Florida, had new Reagan-style Republican governors who would support good welfare reform, and most importantly, Republicans now controlled both the U.S. House and Senate. Since President Clinton had made "the end of welfare as we know it" a mantra of his 1992 campaign, the new Congress could send him true welfare reform and test his promise.

The new Republican Congress in 1994 offered the greatest opportunity in a generation to reverse welfare federalization. The original "Contract with America" welfare-reform plank consisted of many negative mandates that had been the staple of conservative welfare reform over the years because Democratic Congresses would never repeal the open-ended entitlement nature of AFDC.

With the new Congress now in control, I went to the leaders and urged them to think more boldly about reforming welfare. As I saw it, instead of going for a "base hit" we had the bases loaded and could hit a home run by adding an outright repeal of the sixty-year-old Aid to Families with Dependent Children (AFDC) program and replacing it with finite annual appropriations (block grants) to the states. We would reverse the incentives that had always driven greater welfare spending. Under a block-grant approach, a state that required work and removed non-needy families from the rolls would get to keep the federal money saved instead of losing it. This would prove to be a powerful incentive.

The Conservatives Disagree

A debate arose among conservatives over how much freedom the states should have. Led by Senator John Ashcroft (R-MO), some argued for a "no-strings-attached" approach, under which there would be minimal federal requirements on state use of block-grant funds.

Other Senate Republicans wanted the federal government to impose what they saw as a conservative version of welfare, replacing the current liberal one. Under this "strings-attached" approach, the federal government would detail how states could use the block grant funds. This view ultimately prevailed in the House of Representatives, whose welfare reform bill included many pages of federal mandates on states' welfare programs.

Which side was right? Let's take a closer look.

Robert Rector, a policy analyst with the Heritage Foundation, argued for federal controls. He believed that states receiving "free" money from Washington had no incentives to spend it wisely. He wrote,

> When state bureaucracies and governors receive federal money, they treat it like anything else that is free. We all know that politicians spend other people's money unwisely. If there's anything less frugal than a politician spending other people's money, it's one set of politicians with no accountability spending money raised by another set of politicians.

Rector also insisted that without federally imposed rules welfare reform would be sabotaged by welfare bureaucrats at state and local levels—people who he believed had no sympathy with the goals of welfare reform. He claimed that "the bulk of the liberal welfare bureaucracy in the welfare state is in America's state capitals. It is not in Washington."

Opponents to this line of reasoning, including me, argued that when states were given a block grant, the money should be theirs alone. If they wasted it, they would have to use more of their own funds to make up the difference. If they spent it efficiently, they would need to use less of their own money and might have been able to lower taxes. Consequently, states had ideal incentives to use the unrestricted block grant funds efficiently.

In the past, when conservatives took over a state, the Washington bureaucracy stymied their efforts at reform. That is what happened when Governor Reagan and other governors sought to establish workfare in the 1970s. No-strings-attached block grants would eliminate the control of the liberal federal bureaucracy and allow reformers to focus on the state bureaucracies.

I knew firsthand how bureaucrats could thwart attempts to tighten eligibility. As an example, the House welfare reform bill sought to end subsidies for illegitimacy by eliminating AFDC benefits for unmarried mothers under eighteen, except when the pregnancy was due to rape or incest. This was a reasonable objective, but it would not work. Why? Because during the Carter administration, when Congress had attempted to prohibit the use of Medicaid funds for abortions except in cases of rape or incest, federal regulators responded by declaring *all pregnant women under eigh-*

teen the victims of statutory rape. The same clever techniques would nullify the new reforms proposed by the House.

Block grants without strings would allow each state to redesign its welfare program completely. Failed programs needed to be thoroughly reformed and replaced. Thirty years of experience had proved that Washington had no workable welfare solution. There were no good arguments for giving Washington more time—or more authority over welfare.

No Strings, Please

Many welfare reforms advanced inside the Beltway by conservatives and liberals alike were poorly reasoned. While they sounded tough, they were in fact toothless. For example, the House bill and other legislative proposals advanced by conservatives would have cut off at least some welfare assistance after two or five years. But if single welfare mothers and their children remained needy after the cutoff period, does anyone believe that the government would not provide further assistance? Of course not!

The "no-strings" approach to block grants had two major advantages. First, clean block grants would allow the states to experiment with various approaches and determine by experience which ones worked best. The most successful would be copied by others. The most aggressive states would be able to try the most radical reforms, reforms far more innovative than any Congress would ever enact.

Second, block grants with minimal restrictions would allow states to allocate available funds to the most urgent and productive use. Moreover, governors and state legislatures would no longer be able to hide behind federal mandates. If they did not adopt the most effective and least costly reforms, they would be voted out of office.

From my point of view, the Senate reform bill developed by Senate Finance Chairman Bob Packwood (R-OR) was better than the House reform bill. The Packwood bill eliminated most of the unnecessary federal requirements in the House bill, bringing the reforms much closer to no-strings-attached block grants, with the inherent advantages described above. While the Packwood bill was sharply criticized for its lack of federal requirements regarding work and illegitimacy, it allowed states to pursue what each of them considered the best strategy to require work and counter illegitimacy.

The Packwood approach was more likely to achieve passage, since it would not be stalled by debates over various federal requirements. The House bill, by contrast, had already generated considerable opposition because it simply cut off unwed mothers under age eighteen.

However, the best proposal was the one sponsored by Senator Ashcroft. It would eliminate all federal requirements except civil rights nondiscrimination standards. Assistance could only be provided in return for work from able-bodied adults in the family, and the states would be free to determine how to carry this out. In addition, the block-grant funds were paid to the state *directly* by the treasury department rather than through the Department of Health and Human Services. So the liberal federal welfare bureaucracy would be bypassed completely—the resulting block grants truly would go to the states with no strings attached!

Unity at Last?

The deadlock was potentially broken by a plan embracing goals sought by conservatives for twenty-five years. Incredibly, it had the bipartisan endorsement of all fifty of the nation's governors.

Governors Tommy Thompson, John Engler, and Mike Leavitt brilliantly orchestrated the unanimity of the governors behind a program that would achieve 90 percent or more of the block-grant goals sought by the Reagan administration. These block grants would allow states to completely redesign their own welfare programs. They would remove the entire federal bureaucracy from welfare policy and allow voters to hold their own state's government directly responsible for welfare.

The most conservative states would then be free to experiment with the most conservative welfare reforms. Once their successes were demonstrated, political and economic competition among the states would force the others to adopt those reforms as well. The liberal establishment recognized this for the deadly threat to them that it was. They claimed that it would create a "race to the bottom."

Then, remarkably, at the start of the new Republican Congress in 1995, a consensus in favor of the longstanding conservative position arrived. This formerly impossible Reaganite position was embraced by the House and Senate leadership, as well as the Republican governors who now controlled most of the states.

Complications on the Right

Robert Rector had other ideas. He was sure he had the right solutions for welfare policy and he wanted the federal government to *impose* them on every state, rather than restoring state control through block grants. He was right that illegitimacy and family breakdown were the overwhelming problems that needed to be addressed. He advocated a family cap prohibiting increased welfare for recipients that had additional children, and an end to direct cash assistance for teenage welfare moms. While these seemed desirable goals, they could not become the be-all and end-all of welfare policy. It was clear, furthermore, that Rector-style reform legislation could not overcome liberal opposition in Congress and President Clinton's veto.

Rector denounced anyone who supported legislation that would *allow* rather than *require* states to adopt these reforms. He accused them of giving up on marriage and ignoring illegitimacy. Misleading major social conservative groups with both falsehoods and bad judgment, he was able to stop some Republicans from embracing the state-based approach, which is what conservatives had been fighting for all along. If he succeeded in his agenda, he would kill the best prospect conservatives ever had for achieving their welfare reform goals.

This was exactly what Rector was threatening to do with the governors' welfare reform proposal. Ironically, there was only one relevant difference in that plan and the welfare bill passed by the House, which Rector supported. The House bill *required* the family cap but allowed states to opt out of it if they desired. The governors' plan didn't require the cap but *allowed* states to adopt it if they desired.

For that relatively insignificant difference—a difference essential to achieve passage of the bill—Rector was willing to scrap the whole reform effort. He publicly denounced the governors' plan, saying that they refused "to acknowledge or mention the collapse of marriage and the rise of illegitimacy." He said, "The rise in illegitimacy and collapse of marriage do not merit even a token comment . . . from the governors." He added, "The governors' plan blithely ignores . . . the catastrophic rise in illegitimacy."

These were outright falsehoods. The governors' plan endorsed the findings of the Republican reform plan passed by Congress, which included three single-spaced pages about the central problem of illegitimacy and marital breakdown. Those findings stated that "marriage is the foundation of a successful society," recited the problems caused by soaring illegitimacy, and concluded, "It is the view of the Congress that prevention of out-of-wedlock pregnancy and reduction in out-of-wedlock births are very important government interests, and the policy contained in [this bill] is intended to address the crisis." Similarly, the governors endorsed the purposes section of the bill that stated as a prime object to "prevent and reduce the incidence of out-of-wedlock pregnancies and establish annual numerical goals for preventing and reducing the incidence of these pregnancies."

Rector also claimed, "Few, if any, governors have made reducing illegitimacy a central theme of reform." Yet thirteen states had enacted Rector's family cap, and seven other states had received federal permission to adopt it. Approval of family caps through the federal waiver process, however, was slow, with the federal bureaucrats generally imposing expensive conditions.

Enter Bill Clinton and the Election of '96

I strongly opposed Rector's view and recommended that Congress enact the governors' plan without change to maximize pressure on Mr. Clinton and avoid any excuse for a veto. This meant an outright repeal of AFDC, replacing it with finite appropriations to the states with only a requirement of work for welfare. The states would get only the finite block grant but they could design their own programs with no federal eligibility requirements except work and they would get to keep what they saved. We would reverse the perverse incentives of the then present system.

This key element was added to the welfare reform contained in the "Contract with America." The bill was passed twice and vetoed twice by President Clinton.

There were forces that did not want to send the bill back to Clinton for a third time—they wanted to use his vetoes to beat him over the head in the 1996 presidential campaign.

I argued that if they didn't send it to him again, he'd claim that he would have signed the version that the governors had approved—but if they did send it and he signed it we would have truly reformed welfare.

We were too close to not try again. I pushed for minor changes to make it conform to the specific language that the fifty governors had agreed to and I urged congressional leaders to send the bill to the president again. I calculated that Clinton would sign it this time to deprive Republican senator Bob Dole of the issue. I was right.

With his hopes for reelection less than three months away, Clinton folded his hand and signed the Personal Responsibility and Work Opportunity Reconciliation Act on August 22, 1996. This forced him to keep his promise to the American people to "end welfare as we know it" in a way never intended by him when he made the promise. In spite of what he claimed at the time, the bill he signed had all the significant elements that were in the bills he had vetoed.

10

"The Era of Big Government Is Over"

The Welfare Reform of 1996 reversed sixty-one years of U. S. welfare policy, ending a recipient's entitlement to a welfare check. It was a good start, one on which the Congress and the state legislatures could build a better future for millions of people trapped in the old welfare system.

Now states received a finite block grant with few strings attached, giving them new opportunities to solve their welfare problems in their own way. Critics contended that ending the entitlement and giving states more control over their welfare programs would harm the poor. But the truth was, by giving states the freedom to meet the needs of their poor, the new legislation helped to break the cycle of poverty.

While the legislative debate centered on specifics such as work requirements, family caps, and teenage out-of-wedlock births, the real reform was much more revolutionary: *an end to the entitlement status of the open-ended New Deal welfare program Aid to Families with Dependent Children (AFDC).*

The new law eliminated many of the perverse incentives inherent in the old system. In the past, the federal government matched what a state spent on its poor. The more a state would spend, the more money it received. If a state saved a dollar by being more efficient or cutting waste or undeserving recipients, it was penalized by losing a dollar in federal matching funds. *So the states had an incentive to waste money, because they paid only half the cost of wasting a dollar, or conversely, received only half the benefit of saving a dollar.*

Now that the matching-funds approach was replaced by a finite block grant, states could use their resources in the most efficient and effective manner; a dollar saved would not mean a dollar lost.

Besides reversing the entitlement philosophy and restructuring incentives, the legislation established work as the essential element in reform. But it provided the states with enough flexibility to shape welfare reform to fit their particular needs:

- Federal eligibility standards and benefit-level requirements were repealed so that states could determine who was eligible for family welfare and what each person or family would get.
- States had to require work as a condition for receiving any benefits.
- Eligibility and benefit requirements for food stamps were tightened.

- States could take into consideration food stamps received by a family when determining any additional cash benefit needed, thus eliminating duplication.
- States could use religious nonprofit or for-profit entities to carry out welfare reform.
- States could provide welfare benefits in the form of wage supplements to businesses that employed welfare recipients.
- States could refuse benefits for additional children born to a woman who was receiving benefits (the family cap).

Because each welfare recipient is different, welfare reform decisions, like medical diagnoses, require close contact with individuals and families. To the extent the new welfare reform bill moved these decisions out of Washington and back to the states, it was a step in the right direction. Indeed, moving the decisions to the local level—and then to the individual taxpayer—would make welfare reform even better.

Dealing with the Strings

Unfortunately, the welfare legislation also came with a number of unnecessary restrictions. For example, the legislation imposed a five-year limit on welfare benefits, possibly conveying the impression that recipients had an entitlement to five years of welfare. This impression made it easier to criticize efforts of states like Wisconsin, which imposed a two-year limit.

Further, some of the strings were counterproductive. For example, the bill provided money for sexual abstinence education in the public schools. While teaching children abstinence is beneficial, *allowing bureaucrats to interpret and teach it is not.* There is simply no good reason to require *any* type of sex or abstinence education at taxpayer expense.

Nevertheless, the 1996 welfare reform was at least 85 percent of Ronald Reagan's dream, and as he said many times, "Give me 80 percent of what I want this year and I will go back and get the other 20 percent next year."

Dealing with the Welfare Establishment

In the meantime, we had fifty tough jobs on our hands. The enemies of true welfare reform were gearing up to ensure that the 1996 reform would fail—or would be perceived to fail. These enemies were the bureaucrats in the federal and state welfare agencies. They were elected officials in Congress and in the state legislatures. They were "experts" in the media and in many "nonpartisan" think tanks and institutions. They represented the welfare industry and closet socialists who saw AFDC as their long-held vehicle to establish an efficient system for redistributing income.

These enemies of true welfare reform developed "goals and objectives" for defining their version of welfare reform at the state level. These goals would be expansionary, and they would be geared to "break the bank" of block-grant funds so the states would have to go back to Congress "hat in hand," appealing for a return to the old entitlement system. Their allies in institutions such as the Urban Institute would develop systems to measure the success or failure of state efforts, based on *their* definition of welfare reform. Governors would be confronted with seemingly supportive state welfare bureaucracies that would do everything in their power to sabotage successful reform.

"We don't have time," the bureaucrats would say; or, "We tried that and it didn't work;" or, "It will cost more money to do it right;" or, "I recommend that we ask for an extension of time;" or, "Let's just cut the benefits across the board." If a governor heard any of these statements from his welfare department, I would recommend that the bureaucrat be fired or transferred—better yet, contract welfare reform out entirely to an entity dedicated to true reform.

As the French statesman Georges Clemenceau once said, "War is too important to be left to the generals." Well, Governor Ronald Reagan said in 1971 that welfare reform is too important to be left to social workers. He was right.

The new law became effective on October 1, 1996. That meant that the federal funds would be finite and limited after that date. Most states were not ready, because their welfare bureaucracies did not believe that President Clinton would permit true welfare reform. That, of course, was no excuse. Many of us in and out of Congress had been telling them since late 1995 that welfare reform was coming, but most did not move. It was not necessarily the fault of the governors; they were the ones who asked for this welfare reform on Ronald

Reagan's eighty-fifth birthday, February 6, 1996. What could the governors do now? They could call for special sessions. They could put the state legislators on the spot before election day. They could prove that they were serious about the public demands for welfare based on work and an end to policies that encouraged illegitimacy. As Russell Long once told me, "If you want good welfare reform, do it in an election year; Democrats move right."

I wasn't just going to sit still in late 1996, not when we were on the verge of making welfare reform work. I decided to organize a project to call together experienced welfare policy experts in whom I had confidence. They were to determine the specific elements of true welfare reform at the state level. I suggested some principles for the project:

- Able-bodied welfare applicants must take any legitimate job that is offered, when offered.
- Able-bodied people must work first in order to receive any welfare benefit; benefits will be earned before the money flows.
- Child care for other welfare mothers shall be provided, to the extent possible, by welfare mothers who have been proven to be good caretakers as a means of earning their welfare grants.
- No additional benefits shall be provided to families that have additional children while on welfare.
- No benefits will go directly to single mothers under the age of eighteen; benefits will go only through a responsible adult or care-giving entity.

- Benefits and the hours worked to earn them will be provided or recorded through a "smart card" that can be used only by the recipient: no cash or checks and no negotiable food stamps.

- In large or diverse states, such as New York and California, AFDC should be repealed at the state level, and, using the same arguments we used in moving welfare from the federal to the state level, we should support a requirement that welfare eligibility and benefit-level decisions be made by the counties.

- States should determine which nonprofit and religious organizations within the state provide real welfare benefits to poor people and permit tax credits for contributions to those entities for direct welfare purposes. The block grant to each county could then be reduced by the total amount of these contributions within the county. This would encourage healthy competition between county workers and private nonprofits. (Some of the foregoing general policies could be included in the state law block granting the federal and state monies to the counties.)

- Success should be measured by how many persons leave the welfare rolls, not by how many are added—and that of those remaining, that they are earning their benefits or in rehabilitation to the extent possible. Most persons who are not able-bodied are able to do limited kinds of work.

- And the program should be financed within the amount received from the federal government and within the 75 percent state maintenance of effort required in the legislation. Success should not stop at 75 percent. If a state can do the job for less than that, the "penalty" is really a benefit to the federal taxpayer; the federal block grant would simply be reduced by an equivalent amount.

We were entering a critical time. During the days and months ahead we would need to develop the framework for real state welfare reform and provide the means to track and measure state-by-state progress. States had to feel the pressure to act soon, and the governors had to become aware of the enemies of welfare reform: the welfare bureaucrats, liberal institutions, and the media.

In a policy brief for the National Center for Policy Analysis, I called on governors, legislators, and financial officers overseeing welfare reform to recognize the tendency of entrenched welfare forces to defend the status quo. I advised state reformers to answer the old welfare establishment by doing the following.

Challenging federal intrusion. The spirit behind the welfare legislation is to encourage bold new state action and limit federal control. However, federal bureaucrats who have been conditioned to "grow the welfare system" may attempt to assert themselves in state affairs. Governors should challenge this federal intrusion whenever it appears.

Turning to those with innovative welfare ideas. Governors and legislators should give the authority to design the new welfare programs to persons not wedded to the current system.

Expanding devolution. Following the federal reform example, states should repeal their own AFDC programs and state bureaucracies, and send welfare block grants to the counties.

Utilizing the private sector. States should provide a dollar-for-dollar income tax credit to those who want to give part of their state income tax to private and religious nonprofit agencies. This approach, known as "taxpayer choice," would create a level playing field between public- and private-sector charities, with taxpayers deciding which charities deserve the funds. The welfare block grant in each county would be reduced by the amount of money taxpayers in that county decided to allocate to private charities.

Integrating welfare programs. Unfortunately the Food Stamp, Medicaid, and Supplemental Security Income for the Disabled (SSID) programs were not block granted to the states. Through block granting, these programs could be integrated into the states' new welfare systems, as under special waivers Oregon was utilizing with wage supplements and Wisconsin was using with Medicaid.

"Limitation on Federal Authority"

Though the successful implementation of national welfare reform remained to be seen, the states did have one key protection against federal encroachment: Section 417 of the welfare reform act. This section may become as significant historically as the Tenth Amendment to the Constitution, which reserved power to the states.

Section 417 is short and clear. It is entitled "Limitation on Federal Authority," and it reads as follows: "No officer or employee of the Federal Government may regulate the conduct of States under this part or enforce any provision of this part, except to the extent expressly provided in this part." This "part" refers to the Temporary Assistance to Needy Families (TANF) program. Section 417 was placed in the bill at the urging of those of us who anticipated efforts by President Clinton and his departments to "repeal" welfare reform by executive order or regulation after the 1996 election.

At the Democratic National Convention that summer, the president promised Senator Pat Moynihan and others who opposed his signature on the historic legislation that he would do just that after he was reelected. In 1997, he kept his promise, through executive orders and Department of Labor regulation.

Many of the nation's governors cried foul and demanded legislation to overturn the president's actions.

But in fact, the legislation was already on the books. The president and the governors alike either did not know about or simply ignored Section 417.

In August, I requested the highly respected Pacific Legal Foundation to research the 1996 welfare reform act, especially Section 417. A study was prepared for PLF by my old ally John Findley. Findley's study concluded that "[t]his prohibition applies on its face not only to officers and employees of the executive branch but also to members of the judicial branch." Therefore, the president, the secretary of labor and the federal courts, being officers of the federal government, were precluded from acting in the TANF program except where specifically directed to do so, such as in civil rights matters.

Nevertheless, legal opinions circulated Capitol Hill with the finding that federal courts traditionally supported executive branch regulations and executive orders as the best way of interpreting unclear legislation. These opinions either overlooked or ignored Section 417, which broke new ground in federal-state relations. I know of no other instance in federal law where a section like 417 exists.

Opponents of "workfare" were eager to have that element of the welfare reform undone. But Section 417 was clear and specific: the states were to ignore the clearly illegal attempts of the Clinton administration to block workfare.

Workfare, or "work experience training," teaches job skills and habits to people who have never been required to show up on time, to follow orders, to dress properly, or to complete a work shift. In other words, Workfare makes people acceptable candidates for real jobs. For those with a job history, it keeps them ready for another job when it becomes available. Work experience training was not subject to existing labor laws which apply to employees in regular jobs. Section 417, however, made establishing that point unnecessary. That was what Congress intended when they inserted it in the welfare reform legislation. The president accepted it when he ended "welfare as we know it" on August 22, 1996, by signing the legislation.

If governors acted swiftly to implement work experience training, they could expect lawsuits, and they would win them. State welfare departments did not need to wait for federal direction, as they had been accustomed to doing for over sixty years. But many state welfare officials were like the canary that does not fly away when his cage is opened.

So it was up to voters in the states to prod the state bureaucrats into action. They could no longer hide behind the federal welfare bureaucracy. Polls showed that Americans demanded that able-bodied adult welfare recipients get jobs or earn their benefits through work experience. The federal government could no longer dictate how it was to be done. Some states would have to lead the way. The citizens of states that failed to act would eventually realize that they needed new officials.

Section 417 is simple but forceful. It should be included in all legislation that moves authority and responsibility from the federal to the state level. In the states, welfare reform should be carried further by moving authority and responsibility to local levels of government through finite appropriations and state versions of Section 417. If this is done, Thomas Jefferson and Ronald Reagan's trust in the people and local government will be vindicated.

Conclusion

The Way Forward

The facts are in: the welfare reform of 1996 worked. The nation's welfare rolls were cut in half and millions of mothers were self-supporting and free of dependency. The program's cost has remained steady instead of growing each year. The dire predictions of the "welfare experts" did not come to pass. The states proved they can be trusted to do the job, and they have been freed of increasing dependency on federal funding of family welfare. Years after enactment, welfare reform has been recognized as a historic success.

Did reform work because of the employment requirements? Only partly. States were able to require work since 1981. Did it work because of the lifetime five-year limit for welfare? Not really. The good results were coming in before five years was reached. Was it because of the booming economy? Not at all. In every good economic year, from World War II until the mid-1990s, the nation's welfare rolls went up instead of down. Why then did it work? It worked because incentives to the states were turned on their heads.

Let's review the facts.

The 1935 Aid to Families with Dependent Children (AFDC) program was an open-ended entitlement program financed at least in half by the federal government, with the states determining the benefit levels and many other eligibility requirements. Federal money flowed automatically for whatever a state wished to spend on AFDC. Therefore, in good economic years, the states had more money to spend, so they simply made more people eligible for welfare. They did nothing to move able-bodied people off the system. To do so would have been to "lose" federal money.

The result was the exploding welfare rolls of the '60s, '70s, and '80s. During this period the nation's family welfare rolls went down only twice: in 1974 and in 1982, both during major recessions. The 1974 reduction came about through the Reagan California welfare reform of 1971–72, followed by the New York reforms, and later by many other states that followed suit.

We withstood slings and arrows of charges that we were losing federal money. "No," we replied, "we are *saving* federal money." Later, with Governor Reagan's approval, I advised Governor Nelson Rockefeller of New York, who took similar actions. Then, in 1973, as U.S. Commissioner of Welfare, and at Secretary Weinberger's request, I carried the California message to the other states. The result was the historic drop of the nation's AFDC rolls in 1974, the first time since the start of World War II. The 1974 drop came in the middle of a deep recession. Contrary to our opponents' charges, there were no starving children on the street because of the reforms. The reforms affected only the non-needy families, and in most cases the truly needy families benefited from the savings by having their benefits increased.

The reduction of the rolls in 1982, another recession year, was due to President Reagan's comprehensive welfare reforms, which tightened eligibility requirements and were contained in the 1981 Budget Reconciliation Act enacted over the opposition of the House leadership. In addition, the 1981 reforms permitted the states for the first time to *require* work for benefits. Few states took advantage of work requirements, since to remove families from the rolls would result in a "loss" of federal money. Again, there were no starving children thrown on the streets, because the tightened eligibility requirements affected only the non-needy families.

Still, the perverse incentive—the notion that more federal money rolled in when a state spent more—remained. The boom years of the '80s and early '90s saw an exponential growth in the welfare rolls. With new Reagan-style governors, such Wisconsin's Tommy Thompson, determined to reduce their rolls, and using the work requirements permitted in the Reagan reforms of 1981, gains were made in the early '90s.

But the real revolution came after President Clinton signed, under heavy pressure, the welfare reform bill of 1996.

Work requirements? They were very weak in the legislation, but the states now had an incentive to use them. The same was true of the five-year limit. There were many loopholes to protect those families who, through no fault of their own, needed more years. The economy? Now that the states had a financial incentive to get able-bodied people off welfare, the good economy was being used to reduce the rolls, not increase them.

The old welfare system rewarded waste and abuse. It encouraged the states to add millions of non-needy families to the welfare rolls. Worse, it gave them the incentive to hold them there. The new system reversed these incentives and gave the states the ability to use their savings to increase benefits to truly needy families and to create "rainy day" funds for when the economy turned bad. Now, welfare rolls would go up in bad times and down in good times. Unlike the old AFDC program, which ensured that the rolls would go up in bad times and continue up at an accelerated rate in good times.

Welfare reform succeeded because we reversed the incentives to the states. We stopped the uncontrolled growth in welfare spending. We let the states have their reward for doing a good job reforming their welfare program. If this promise was kept, the governors would be more apt to support capping and block granting other open-ended welfare entitlement programs.

Now that the facts are in on welfare reform's success, it is time to take the next steps. We need to free the states from their increasing dependency on federal funding for the other open-ended welfare entitlement programs.

In 2003, I proposed using the states to follow up on family welfare reform by giving them the authority, responsibility, and financial incentives to reform the other major welfare programs—Medicaid, food stamps, and Supplemental Security Income for the Disabled (SSID). All are open-ended entitlement programs; all contain much waste, fraud, and abuse.

Solution for Medicaid

Medicaid should not be confused with Medicare. Medicaid provides health care for welfare families and for persons who are on welfare because of their age or disability and have little or no income. Medi*care* is a health-care insurance program for the employed or retired after they reach the age of sixty-five or become disabled. They have contributed to Medicare throughout their working life with mandatory withholdings from their wages.

Medicare is administered by the federal government. Medicaid is administered by the states and paid for by an open-ended federal-state matching program. The governors scream for increased federal matching for Medicaid spending. This would be the worst way to go. Federal matching simply generates more, not less, state spending, since the more the state spends, the more federal money flows in.

The solution, as with family welfare, is to replace Medicaid with finite block grants to the states, to give the states a financial incentive to ensure that waste is reduced or eliminated. Federal mandates should be removed or reduced to give states the ability to design systems to meet their individual needs. The money they save will stay in the state as a reserve against bad times or be used for other necessary state health needs.

Controlling Food Stamps

The Food Stamp Program is worse. The federal government pays the full cost of food stamps and the states administer the program, paying half of the administrative costs. There is no incentive to eliminate fraud and abuse, since all the money saved is federal money and it costs the state money to administer antifraud and antiwaste programs.

In addition, the federal government sets eligibility standards and benefit levels that may not be synchronized with state standards for their family cash welfare programs.

The food industry strongly defends the Food Stamp Program, and we need not do away with food stamps. However, instead of remaining an open-ended entitlement program for individuals, it should be replaced with finite block grants of stamps to the states, with eligibility and benefit requirements set by the state as they do now with family welfare. Instead of sending a check, the federal government can deposit a truckload of food stamps in the state each month and let the state decide how to distribute them. The savings from the fraud and abuse that is eliminated stays within the state, giving the state a strong incentive to see that the stamps go only to those who need them.

Ending SSID Fraud

The third program that should be reformed is the Supplemental Security Income Program for the Disabled (SSID). This is the program for people who are too disabled to work and have little or no income.

In 1971, when I was welfare director for Governor Reagan, the states still administered this program. I found that throughout California nondisabled people were being admitted to the welfare rolls. It was particularly bad in the Haight-Asbury district of San Francisco, where hippie doctors were issuing papers declaring their counterculture friends disabled. We conducted a complete review of the cases throughout the state and cleaned the rolls.

In 1973, however, the Nixon administration moved SSID from state to federal administration, with some states adding supplements to the federal grants. Knowing when someone is actually disabled and the degree of disability was difficult at best, but it certainly could not be done accurately at the national level. According to the requirement, a disability was expected to last for at least a year, but often, disability ended and people remained on the rolls.

It was reported that, indeed, some states moved their family welfare recipients to the federal disability rolls, when in fact the people were not truly incapable of supporting themselves. In addition, SSID recipients were automatically eligible for Medicaid, for which the states were financially obligated to pay half the cost.

The states were handling SSID quite well until it was removed from them in 1973. Congress should provide SSID in block grants to the states, just as it did with family welfare. Much of the fraud and abuse can be detected and eliminated by the states and their counties, which are much closer to the people than the federal government. The money saved can stay within the state to be used for other pressing needs for disabled people.

Ten years after the 1996 reforms, the evidence is unmistakable. By ending the idea of entitlement to welfare and replacing it with finite block grants, the states were responsible, rolls have plummeted, and 2.5 million families escaped the cycle of poverty and are self supporting. Dire predictions by opponents of welfare reform that the states would "race to the bottom," and that a million children would be starving in the streets, proved false. States are responsible because they care about the welfare of their people.

Now that that argument is over, we should build on this success by doing the same with the three remaining welfare entitlement programs. It could be made voluntary for each state, but states that do not take it should not receive additional federal funding. Any governors or state legislators who do not accept the challenge would be sending a message to its voters that they are afraid to accept the responsibility. Doubtless, other citizens more willing and able to do so would contest them in the next election.

I predict that most governors will oppose block-granting these programs because they don't want the responsibility of cutting out waste and taking the heat for it. But they should follow Ronald Reagan's example: He took the heat in welfare reform, he succeeded, and he was elected president.

The national welfare reform of 1996 was the culmination of a dream of Ronald Reagan's and mine that stretched back to 1971.

The states now have a real incentive to use work requirements to move people into jobs and keep the money they save by doing so. Welfare now works as intended: Rolls go up in bad times and down in good times, instead of up and up in bad *and* good times.

No other government in the world was established by independent states and grown by adding states with the same authority as the original thirteen. Each state has a chief executive, and a legislature elected by its citizens, and a court system responsible to its people. They have power to raise taxes and pass all laws not in conflict with the Constitution.

The states are close to the people. When it comes to administering welfare, the states are in a much better position to determine need, enforce work requirements, and determine disability.

When welfare reform was about to be enacted in 1996, Senator Daniel Patrick Moynihan and the Urban Institute predicted that "within a year there will be a million children starving in the streets," and that states will engage in a "race to the bottom." My challenge to that charge was to please tell me which governor and which legislature would turn their poor children onto the streets? Years have now passed, and no governor or legislature has done so. Federalism works. And for demonstrating that great American fact yet again, we have Ronald Reagan to thank.

EDITORS' EPILOGUE

Bob Carleson lived to see the result of his twenty-five years of reforming welfare exceed even his dreams. But until his passing in April 2006, he was on guard and fought to protect it. He knew that the enemies of true welfare reform would seek every opportunity to return to the old federally controlled system that had enslaved generations into poverty. His mantra became "if it ain't broke, don't fix it."

Sadly, in February 2009 Congress and the president quietly "fixed" welfare reform as part of the massive stimulus package. They effectively undid all of the successful elements of the 1996 welfare reform that freed tens of millions of Americans from the shackles of dependence.

It is beyond question that welfare reform succeeded. As Robert Samuelson wrote in the *Washington Post* in

2006, "A decade later, [welfare reform] stands as a rarity: a Washington success story."

But now the stage has been set to reinstitutionalize poverty and rob America's most vulnerable children of opportunity. Undoing the 1996 welfare reform will prove to be the cruelest act of the American government in our time.

Appendix

Statement by
the Honorable Ronald Reagan
Governor of California
to
Senate Finance Committee

February 1, 1972

Mr. Chairman, members of the Committee, I appreciate the opportunity to testify here today—particularly since I have never before had this privilege and honor—and also because I consider the welfare problem the gravest domestic issue our Nation faces.

Two years ago welfare was out of control nationally and California was no exception. At that time HR 16311, and later HR 1, were presented as a solution to the problem. One of its authors responded publicly to a critical question by answering that "It's better than sitting on our hands and doing nothing."

I share the President's desire to reform welfare and certainly share his belief that there should be a restoration of the work ethic. However, as you are aware, I have had some very serious reservations about several of the approaches to welfare reform embodied in HR 1.

In August 1970 I presented to this Committee a statement regarding the version of HR 16311 which was pending before your Committee. Many of the provisions of that Bill to which I objected in my statement are in HR 1.

My remarks today will concentrate on six areas of major concern I have with HR 1 and with the need for federal action in achieving real welfare reform. I believe that:

1. States are better equipped than the federal government to administer effective welfare reforms if they are given broad authority to utilize administrative and policy discretion.

2. A system of a guaranteed income, whatever it may be called, would not be an effective reform of welfare, but would tend to create an even greater human problem.

3. A limit should be set on the gross income a family can receive and still remain eligible for welfare benefits.

4. For all those who are employable, a requirement be adopted that work in the community be performed as a condition of eligibility for welfare benefits without additional compensation.

5. The greatest single problem in welfare today is the

breakdown of family responsibility. Strong provision should be made to insure maximum support from responsible absent parents.

6. A simplified system of pensions should be established for the needy aged, blind, and the totally and permanently disabled.

In August of 1970 the size and cost of welfare had grown into a monster which was devouring many of California's programs and was failing to meet the needs of those who, through no fault of their own, have nowhere else to turn but to government for subsistence. We didn't just become aware of this problem in 1970 but our earlier efforts to deal with it weren't too successful; perhaps because we relied on professional welfare experts to propose solutions and all too often they were more familiar with what they were sure they could not do, so the situation became worse instead of better. Finally, to avert a fiscal and human disaster, I asked several members of my administration, who had proven themselves in other state administrative posts, to form a task force and to devote full time for as long as it took to see if and how real reform of welfare could be developed and implemented. They expanded their task force to include experienced attorneys and other management and fiscal experts from the private sector. These men and women served on a volunteer basis for four months reviewing federal laws, state laws, and federal and state regulations. They interviewed over 700 people involved in administering welfare in California at all levels, and developed proposals and ideas for a realistic and humane reform of welfare.

In early March of 1971, not quite a year ago, we presented the legislature with the most comprehensive proposal for welfare reform ever attempted in California and perhaps the nation. All in all, there were over 70 major points involving administrative, regulatory, and legislative changes.

We had already gone ahead in January with those changes we could make administratively and we continued through the spring and summer until the legislature finally agreed to most of the statutory changes we'd asked for, plus others which were negotiated.

It should be pointed out that we weren't exactly exploring uncharted land. Our task force findings had led to the conclusion that the basic original structure of the welfare system was sound. It was based on a concept of aid to the needy aged, the blind and disabled and to children deprived of parental support. Able-bodied adults were expected to support themselves, their children and their aged parents to the extent of their capabilities. The system was meant to be administered by the states and counties with the federal government sharing the cost.

But we had also learned that, almost from the start, this basic structure had been undermined. Sometimes by federal or state law, but more often by regulations, state and federal. Regulations drawn up by the federal agency administering welfare reflected the philosophy of the permanent employees rather than an interpretation of the law. Thus the original legislative intent was often distorted.

Back in January when we began, there were plenty of experts telling us that no state could reform welfare, that the statutory, regulatory and administrative constraints were too many and too inflexible. Figures now indicate that they were wrong.

According to HEW, national welfare and Medicaid costs combined increased last year by 27 percent. In California, we estimate an increase in welfare and Medicaid costs of only 5.9 percent next year. And that doesn't tell the full story of what has happened and is still happening because of our reforms. We suspect we may be playing it too safe.

For several years up until last April, California's case load increased more than 40,000 persons per month. This held true even when the economy was booming and we had full employment. Our projections were that by this last December we would have added another 495,000 to the rolls. Not only did this not happen, but in December we had 176,000 fewer welfare recipients than we had in March, 1971. In that nine month period we have reduced spending, federal, state and local, by more than $120 million below what it would have been without the reform. Though the December figure increased by a few hundred recipients, it was 60,000 less than the increase in December of 1970, and the lowest December increase in 30 years.

Because of these savings, we have achieved one of our primary goals—we have been able to increase the grants to the truly needy. An AFDC family of four, to cite an example, receiving $221 last spring now receives $280 a month. A cost of living increase was granted in December to the aged, blind and disabled. In the current fiscal year, we will spend $338 million less in federal, state and county funds than would have been necessary without the reform. In our '72–'73 budget I mentioned a moment ago, we are asking for $708 million less than would have been required without reform.

Let me stress once again—the important thing is we didn't find any new magic formula. We simply overhauled the present structurally sound welfare system. We insured adequate aid to the aged, the blind, the disabled, and children who are deprived of parental support and reduced aid to the non-needy with realistic work incentives so that funds could be redirected to the truly needy. Our program requires employable recipients to accept work if offered, and that if jobs are not available, to work in the community in order to remain eligible. Absent fathers are now legally indebted to the county for benefits paid to their families with a provision for wage attachments and property liens, if necessary. Fiscal incentives are provided to help counties trace absent fathers.

But maybe most important is the fact that the California plan retains most of the administration and responsibility for an effective and efficient welfare program at the level closest to those who benefit and those who must pay the bill.

Members of our task force found that with provision for reasonable administrative discretion, combined with fiscal responsibility and discipline, the most effective administrative efforts in California were those carried on in the medium and smaller sized counties. We retained the concept of state supervision and county administration of welfare on a partnership basis.

In spite of our reforms, many of the greatest loopholes which still permit abuse, inhibit effective state action, and which have led to a loss of public confidence, remain in federal law and federal regulations—mainly regulation. We see a fiscal and administrative disaster if the administration of the welfare system is centralized here in Washington as proposed in HR 1. As you've already heard, HEW claims that HR 1 would save California $234 million. Actually, it would increase our costs by nearly $100 million.

We are presently being challenged in court on nine of our eighty four changes on the grounds that we are in violation of federal law. Regardless of the outcome, we believe we are not in violation of Congressional intent before it was reinterpreted in regulations.

To get back to the matter of HR 1, I respectfully urge this Committee to eliminate the proposal to provide welfare benefits to intact families with employed fathers. I am not unaware of nor insensitive to the plight of the low earner but I believe relief to those families can be provided in the form of Social Security and income tax exemptions. It doesn't seem right to reduce a man's take-home pay with taxes and then send him a government dole which robs him of the feeling of accomplishment and dignity which comes from providing for his family by his own efforts. By the same token, we feel that the able-bodied recipient should be given the maximum opportunity to support his family by doing work in his community which will benefit the community. At the same time it develops and maintains his ability to perform effectively in a regular job when it becomes available. We don't suggest this in any punitive way nor are we advocating useless make-work chores. Not only will the individual benefit from participating in useful work, but those who foot the bill will be more apt to approve if they see community services being performed. If I could anticipate a possible question concerning the usefulness of such a community work force let me just mention one of the many possibilities. The Los Angeles school system reported last week that vandalism was costing that one city alone $50 million a year. Night watchmen might change that.

I was pleased to see that the Talmadge amendment to the tax bill was adopted by Congress and signed into law by the President. Most of the features of the Talmadge amendment parallel very closely the "separation of employables" portion of our California welfare reform program. However, many of the so-called work incentives in the present system, and in HR 1 as passed by the House of Representatives, continue to insure aid to the non-needy, and able-bodied adults are not required to work in the community.

We recommend that a realistic and absolute ceiling be placed on the income that a family may have and still be eligible for welfare. The experts tell us on one hand (and I believe them) that all but a few welfare recipients would prefer to work if work or jobs were available. Yet, on the other hand, they tell us that we cannot expect someone to be willing to take a job or go to work if his welfare grant is significantly diminished. These expert opinions obviously are in conflict. I propose a combination of work incentives including a mandatory work requirement and, in the case of a mother-headed family, reasonable child care expenses and a portion of her income could be exempted until she has stabilized her work situation. However, an absolute ceiling on the gross income a family may receive and still be eligible for welfare should be set at 150 percent of the standard of need. The proposed limitation of work-related expenses contained in HR 1 should be retained.

We believe that the present grant sharing ratio between the state and the federal government should be retained. However, since eligibility of 85 percent of the caseload is due to an absent father, real fiscal relief can be provided the states by helping them solve this problem. We propose that the federal government adopt a plan similar to California's which would finance the effort to locate absent fathers and enforce compliance with child-support laws. The best source of funds would be to permit the states or counties to retain 100% of the federal share of grants recovered through collections from absent fathers and through efforts of fraud control units.

I support the concept of a simplified system of pensions for the needy aged, blind, and totally and permanently disabled. Sums of money spent on costly and complicated eligibility and grant determination systems for these categories would be better spent in increasing benefits to these people, many of whom have provided adequately for themselves during their productive and working days, but who have found that inflation has wiped out the fruits of their past accomplishments.

The effectiveness of the states' and counties' administration of welfare has come under heavy criticism and attack. Perhaps in a number of instances this may be justified. However, it is almost impossible to hold a state accountable for effective administrative practices and policies under the present straight jacket of federal statutes, court interpretations, regulations, and abuses of administrative discretion. Give the states the broadest authority to administer the system with proper goals and objectives and then hold us accountable for our effectiveness in meeting these goals and objectives. Senator Curtis's approach in S-2037 to severely constrain the power of federal administrators and return authority to the states is definitely going in the right direction.

I am submitting at this time to you a more detailed listing of amendments that we would offer to HR 1 and urge your favorable consideration of them. They are the product of our experience with an actual reform program that is succeeding in California, they are not theory. I believe that we have demonstrated in California that a responsible approach to reform of the present welfare system is possible and that given tolls, discretion, and adequate financial assistance, states and counties are in the best position to provide a welfare system patterned to meet the real needs of those in America who, through no fault of their own, have nowhere else to turn but to government.

What California has done—other states can do.

Welfare needs a purpose—to provide for the needy of course – but more than that, to salvage these our fellow citizens, to make them self-sustaining and as quickly as possible, independent of welfare. There has been something terribly wrong with a program that grows ever larger even when prosperity for everyone else is increasing.

We should measure welfare's success by how many people leave welfare, not by how many more are added.

Thank you.

Index

A

B

G

H

I

J

K

L

R

S

Y

Z